Tina Bruce

Learning through Play

2nd edition

HODDER
EDUCATION
AN HACHETTE UK COMPANY

Orders: please contact Bookpoint Ltd, 130 Milton Park, Abingdon, Oxon OX14 4SB.
Telephone: (44) 01235 827720. Fax: (44) 01235 400454. Lines are open from 9.00 – 5.00,
Monday to Saturday, with a 24-hour message answering service. You can also order through our
website **www.hoddereducation.co.uk**

British Library Cataloguing in Publication Data
A catalogue record for this title is available from the British Library

ISBN: 978 1 444 137 163

First Edition Published 2001
This Edition Published 2011

Impression number   10 9 8 7 6 5 4 3 2 1
Year   2014, 2013, 2012, 2011

Cover photo © Steve Wisbauer/Digital Vision/Getty Images.
Part 1 section header photo © Darren Baker – Fotolia.com; part 2 section header photo © iofoto – Fotolia.com.
All other photography © Andrew Callaghan, 2010.
Typeset by Pantek Arts Ltd, Maidstone, Kent.
Printed in Italy for Hodder Education, an Hachette UK Company,
338 Euston Road, London NW1 3BH

Contents

Dedication

To Dr Elizabeth Bevan Roberts

A steadfast friend, whose wisdom and gentle humour has sustained me: a catalyst, who quietly but surely helps those working in education to keep going, even when it gets tough.

Acknowledgements

I would like to thank Andrew Callaghan, whose photographs bring alive the practical points and the theory in the book. And at Hodder Education, my thanks go to Gemma Parsons for her work in getting the brief together, Chloé Harmsworth, Viv Church and Colin Goodlad, who has been a tower of strength throughout.

As always, my thanks to Ian Bruce, who is always there for me, and with whom I move into our ruby days.

Introduction

Aim

This book is designed to help adults who spend time with babies, toddlers and children 0–7 years. The focus is on developing learning through play. The aim is to help adults support children so that their play contributes in deep and far-reaching, lasting ways to their lifelong learning during the first years of a child's life, and hopefully beyond. In middle childhood (Bruce, 2011a and b) we now usually refer to play developing into creativity and imaginative, problem-solving pursuits, with hobbies and interests.

Part 1 of the book sets the scene, forming a backdrop to Part 2. Part 2 gives practical ways in which adults can help children to develop their play.

Cultural influences

It is important to remember that play is influenced by cultural setting and atmosphere. This book is rooted in the cultural context of the UK. Currently, in England and other countries of the UK, there is great interest in the education and care of babies and toddlers.

The curriculum framework documents of the four UK countries emphasise the importance of learning through play. It is important not to use these as the first document, but to learn about play and then incorporate the official document into that practice, so that official documents serve to help practitioners reflect as well as to be accountable. Practitioners should use official documents – official documents should not use practitioners.

It is important to remember that human children have the biological possibility to play. It would, therefore, be very unfortunate if this book was about helping only children in the UK to learn through their play. Play is important throughout the world, as young children grow up and learn through engaging in play. It is not the only way in which children learn, but it is an important way.

We shall, therefore, look at how we can help children to learn through their play, using three strands:

1. The traditional early childhood curriculum approach of the pioneers.
2. Developing the tradition into a modern approach using the evidence from research and theory to illuminate practice.
3. The requirements of governments for the early childhood curriculum set out in official framework documents.

> Evidence across the world suggests that it is best for children not to be subjected to early formal teaching. Between six and seven years, children transition into middle childhood. Young children learn through rich, broad and deep first-hand experiences, movement feedback, communication and language, and – important and highlighted in this book – through *play*.

It is vital for those spending time with children during early childhood to understand the importance of play.

This book is designed to help adults spending time with children to see how play begins in babyhood and toddler times, and how to build on basic play. They can then help children to develop more complex free-flowing play (Bruce, 1991) in the first seven years.

It cannot be stressed too strongly that, if adults playing with children at home or in early childhood group settings use the time-honoured principles of the pioneers, updated through current research and theory, the legal requirements for early childhood curriculum framework documents of the four UK countries will be more than fulfilled. This can be demonstrated through a good record-keeping system which shows a child's learning journey.

Summary

At the end of the book, you will find a summary of the main points made in the book. It gives the important points about play, not just in the UK but across time and space.

At the end of each chapter you will find 'Reflective questions for your practice' points to consider and act upon.

This is a book about play in early childhood. If you want to think about children and their development and learning in the larger context, consider *Early Childhood Education*, 4th edition (2011b), a related text by the same author. If you want to explore the relationship between play, creativity and imagination in more depth, a related text is *Cultivating Creativity in Babies, Toddlers and Young Children*, 2nd edition (2011a). A general text is *Child Care and Education*, 5th edition (2010b) by Bruce, Meggitt and Grenier.

1 Setting the scene for learning through play (0–7 years)

Play in babyhood

In everyday life babies inevitably come into contact with people. They need to be changed, fed, washed and clothed. They go with people to the shops, and to meet older brothers and sisters from school. They are cuddled and bounced on people's knees. These are all wonderful opportunities for play. Babies need to spend time with people who encourage and support their play.

Sometimes play will be with people, and sometimes with objects. Play often arises out of situations when parents and babies spend enjoyable times together. For example, in the photographs in Chapter 3, the babies and their mothers are attending a baby massage group.

Babies play using their senses of touch, sight, smell, hearing and taste, and using feedback from their movements. As their physical coordination develops, helped along by the play they engage in, they begin to be able to hold objects, look at things, reach for things and put them in their mouths.

When they learn to let go and release an object, a whole new kind of play opens up. Peekaboo is a huge step forward. The play is enjoyable, but it is also intellectually and emotionally challenging. Trying to work out where something has gone is a puzzle. But seeing an object vanish, just as you thought you were going to hold it, is a bit frustrating. Adults need to be sensitive in play, so that frustration does not take over from enjoyment. When play fades away, so does learning of the deepest kind.

In this book, narrative observation is emphasised. The practitioner gathers a description of the play, then analyses it and uses this to plan how to support the play. Play comes alive as we see it free flowing along through real babies, and in children at home and in early childhood settings.

Play during the toddler years

The toddler period, when children begin to walk and toddle about, is a crucial period for the development of play. It is the time when play has the possibility to develop the defining features which use rehearsal of roles, pretending, imagining and creating play props. During this time, children are beginning to walk, talk and pretend.

This is all part of the symbolic explosion which occurs as the toddler turns into a talker and a player with symbols. You may like to look at the definitions box on page 4, which explains these terms.

Toddlers have strong images of the past and future that allow them to imagine. They are very social and, as they work out their identity (Who am I? Who is me?), they begin to realise that other people are different from them (Who are you?). They can imitate what others do. They take on the role of being someone else, usually by imitating their actions. They do not yet sympathise (empathise) with the role. For example, they will say, 'I ironing for the baby.' This means they may imitate the actions of an adult ironing. But, as yet, they are not deeply in the role of being the character doing the ironing – that will develop later.

Toddlers are beginning to use the symbols of their culture. The iron is a symbol in this play scenario. The toy iron stands for a real one. It allows the toddler to rehearse, quite safely and without being burned, roles that adults take on.

Play in the first seven years

Children from three to seven years of age (and beyond) need:

* people who help them to play
* places to play
* materials for play props.

The role of the adult is crucial in helping children to develop their play. In other cultural contexts, in other parts of the world, play is usually handed on from generation to generation of children, without adult support (Rogoff *et al.*, 1998). For example, older children usually play with younger children, often out of doors. In the South African township, Soweto, a mixed-age group of children play in a den they have made, preparing pretend food. The younger children learn how to do this by being the babies, and the older children make the meals and pretend to feed them. This sort of play can be found all over the world.

Adults or older children can be helpful to children as they play because they:

* observe children at play (as we will see in Chapter 3), in order to be informed about children's learning
* use their observations to support and extend the play by planning and resourcing a challenging environment (e.g. setting up a shop, in the garden (as in Chapters 4 and 6))
* create appropriate play environments which help children to develop and learn through their play
* engage in the play and encourage the development of communication (both non-verbal and spoken) through play
* know when to take a back seat and let children develop the play without invasion or adult domination.

In this book, we shall see examples of children at home and in group settings where they are helped to learn through well-planned and supported play. There is nothing like observing real children for gaining an insight into working with them. The book will, therefore, help parents, childminders and practitioners in group settings to develop play through observation.

Learning through play

Play, like creativity, helps children to make connections in their learning. In Chapter 3 we shall look at the 12 features of free-flow play as a tool for analysing the play. Feature 12 emphasises that play orchestrates learning – it helps children to bring together what they know in a connected and whole way.

Play helps children to be led forward actively in their learning. Extending learning means leading children forward as well as broadening the learning.

However, helping children to play requires the most sophisticated teaching strategies of all. Although the adult leads the child forward, the child must also have the opportunity to reflect on what they have already learned. Children who are encouraged to do this are easier to lead forward. They are easier to teach because, through their play, they have been able to understand and bring meaning to their learning. This means they keep coming back for more!

In each chapter of Part 2, we explore a different way to emphasise the powerful and long-lasting learning which becomes possible when, in their play, children are taught to reflect on what they have learned.

The box below contains definitions which cover some of the phrases you will come across as you read this book.

Definitions

Creativity

The imagination makes images in the mind. Creativity is the process by which children turn these images into creations. They try out ideas, feelings and relationships in their role play or pretend play, make props for their play or find things to be used as play props. They make connections. They might be creative using paint, make music, dance, make constructions in block play, tell or write a story or make models with found materials or clay.

In the context of play, creativity is more of a process than a product. The richer the creative process (the trying out of the imagination), the richer the product (the play scenario, the construction, the song, the dance, etc.).

Free-flow play

Free-flow play arises out of 12 features of play (Bruce, 1991, 2010a, 2010b) which have been identified as important in its development. When the 12 features are considered together, it is possible to assess whether or not the play is of sufficient quality to be called free-flow play. The 12 features are covered in more detail in Chapter 3 and are referred to throughout the book.

Imagination

This is the rearrangement of past experiences in new and fascinating ways (McKellar, 1957). The imagination makes images in the mind about ideas, thoughts, feelings and relationships with the self, others and the universe.

Becoming a symbol user and a symbol maker

The process of becoming a symbol user involves young children, from toddler times onwards, in making one thing stand for another. For example, during play in the garden, a twig might stand for a knife; a leaf might stand for a plate; a mud pie might stand for the cake, which is to be cut. The twig, leaf and mud pie are not really a knife, plate or cake, they are symbols that stand for those things. The child might attend her grandmother's birthday and afterwards play at this scenario. The child is not really the grandmother about to cut the cake on her ninetieth birthday, she is pretending to be the grandmother. She is using symbolic behaviour. The child is a symbol user and a symbol maker.

Summary

This chapter has signalled the importance of bringing together several views of play:

* The traditional view, arising out of the work of late nineteenth- and early twentieth-century pioneers of the early childhood curriculum in the UK, that play is of central importance in helping children to develop and learn.
* Evidence of a modern kind, that play supports and extends children in their development and learning, especially when it is well planned.
* The view of play expressed in the official documents of the four UK countries, Wales, Scotland, Northern Ireland and England.

Bringing together these three strands shows that, whichever way play is approached, it is important in early childhood.

If the first two are valued, because they help us to gain valuable insights and to learn about supporting play, then the third strand will be addressed naturally as a result.

REFLECTIVE QUESTIONS FOR YOUR PRACTICE

Find out more about the views of Friedrich Froebel, who first introduced play into early childhood education.

Find out what Jean Piaget, Lev Vygotsky, Jerome Bruner, Anna Freud, Erik Erikson, Donald Winnicott, Melanie Klein or Susan Isaacs thought about the importance of play.

See: Bruce, T. (2011b) *Early Childhood Education*, 4th edn, Hodder Education: London and Bruce, T., Meggitt, C. and Grenier, J. (2010b) *Child Care and Education*, 5th edn, Hodder Education: London.

What country do you live in? Find out about the official framework that practitioners are either guided to follow or legally required to follow.

Think about how you encourage play. Give three things that are part of your work in encouraging play.

Then look at the official framework document of the country to see if what you are already doing (those three things about play that are part of your practice) connects with this.

Fair play in early childhood practice

Studying play

Most people in the world pay no intellectual attention at all to childhood play. They do not consciously develop it in their children. Families and carers do not spend huge amounts of their time studying the detail of a child's progress in learning to sit, crawl, walk or talk. These things just happen naturally. It is the same with childhood play – it is usually simply thought of as a part of growing up. It is not usual for it to be discussed or studied.

It is only a minority of people who have made childhood play a subject of study. However, those who do study young children at play, and who perhaps even join in with their play, usually find themselves becoming more and more fascinated with how play begins to develop and burgeon in early childhood (under eight years).

The serious study of childhood play began with the pioneers of the early childhood curriculum. (If you want to find out more about the history, read Bruce (2011b) and Bruce, Meggitt and Grenier (2010b).) Friedrich Froebel (1782–1852) introduced the idea that children's play is important for their development and learning, and he made it central to early childhood education. Since then, a world movement has developed and led to an International Charter of Human Rights. This has in it Article 44, which states the child's Right to Play. This is not about giving children time off work, which would be recreation – as we shall see in this book, the right to play is about helping children to learn in the deepest ways possible for their early years of life.

> ### Key message
> Childhood play becomes a resource that remains deep inside the maturing person to be used later in adult life.

Western early childhood education and care

The pioneers

Froebel put the study of childhood play on the Western European map. He took the natural play of children and gave it status. It is of central importance in his philosophy for the education and care of young children. Over the years, he increasingly developed a curriculum around the child's free play, which he came to believe was the highest form of learning.

Froebel's ideas spread across Europe and reached the USA, where kindergartens were also established on a wide scale. In the UK his philosophy of education influenced pioneers such as Margaret McMillan (1860–1931) and Susan Isaacs (1885–1948).

The British nursery schools developed by Margaret McMillan were emulated throughout the world, and still are. Susan Isaacs established the Child Development Department at the University of London in the 1930s. She trained students to observe, describe, analyse, study and develop childhood play. She understood that grounded theory underpins both practice and further theory. This is because gathering data through careful observation informs researchers, who can then build theories of their own.

It is important to note that later, Rudolf Steiner (1861–1925) also gave play a central place in early childhood education. The emphasis is on imaginative play with open-ended materials, logs, pine cones, etc. (Taplin, 2010).

Maria Montessori (1869–1952), however, did not give play a central place in her curriculum. She felt that children prefer to engage in real rather than pretend cooking, for instance. Montessorians today work along the same lines (Montessori Schools Association, 2008). They feel the defining factors are that children have freedom of choice, and the exercise of will and deep engagement, which lead to concentration.

Both Froebel and, later, Steiner would argue, supported by a wealth of research and theory, that play helps children to transform their learning and take it from the immediate here and now, and to use their experience as a resource. Through play they can transform, vary, abstract, develop, imagine, create and innovate as they move into the future. As they do this, they will of course engage, concentrate and have freedom of choice, but they will go beyond the real world as increasingly skilled symbol users and symbol makers. Play lifts children to higher levels of functioning than the everyday experiences such as cooking in which they engage.

Modern Western experts
Cross-cultural issues

The study of play by experts such as Susan Isaacs began in the first half of the twentieth century. It grew from the understanding of child development that emerged from Western Europe and the USA.

In recent years postmodernists have been 'disrupting commonly held "truths" about our understandings of children and how they develop and learn' (Albon, 2010: 38). But it has been useful, as Albon says, to 'look again' at the play of young children and to see that play is still to be valued.

Most children in the world play and this helps them to:

* become symbol users and symbol makers
* think in abstract ways that take them beyond the here and now
* develop theory of mind and decentrate (an understanding of the way others think and feel, and relate to people – see Chapter 7)
* make changes, transforming their lives and events by using their imagination and creating alternative, possible worlds
* be flexible, adaptive thinkers, so that intelligence continues to develop throughout life.

Play is like a reservoir full of water: the deeper the reservoir, the more water can be stored and used in times of drought. Childhood play becomes a resource that remains deep inside the maturing person to be used later in adult life.

The concept of 'play' changes over time, even within one cultural context. Each generation and each culture and society reinterprets the way it regards childhood play.

The human brain has the potential to play

The human brain, unless damaged, is able, from the start of life, to take in experiences of people and objects, places and events. We know that:

* babies need people and real physical experiences in order to develop
* babies are able to use their innate knowledge (the knowledge they are born with) as a means of learning more
* according to Colwyn Trevarthen (1998), babies arrive already equipped to be interested in faces and voices, and with an innate sense of a world with people in it.

Key message
To be a symbol user means being able to make one thing stand for another.

Babies are born to be symbol users

According to researchers such as Gopnik, Meltzoff and Kuhl (1999), babies are self-programmed to learn more than they know when they are born. They learn through experience.

We don't have to motivate babies to become symbol users. To be a symbol user means being able to make one thing stand for something else – the doll stands for the baby. Symbols have the power to help humans of all ages think beyond the here and now. The child might pretend the doll is the baby, alongside a real baby being bathed. However, we often see children pretend a doll is the baby when the real baby is no longer there. They show in their pretend play how they watched the baby being bathed yesterday (past), or that they will help to bath the baby later (future).

Humans arrive as newborns already equipped to develop this ability. The world they experience with people and objects triggers the process to begin developing, so that between two and five years there is typically a symbolic explosion, which shows up in the child's play. The beginning of the ability to play using symbols forms an important part of this symbolic explosion, according to the findings of Western research.

The link between symbols and imagination

Being a symbol user also helps children to become imaginative and creative. Images form in the mind from an early age. Even very young babies remember faces. They have an image of people they love and know well, which means they can recognise family and friends. By about seven months they may even show 'stranger fear' of someone who looks different from the image they have formed of what a human face should look like.

Imagination is about taking images and rearranging them in the mind in new and fascinating ways. Imagination occurs when children go beyond the here and now into the past (recognising) and into the future (rearranging the past into something new and different) (McKellar, 1957). When children play they transform images in this way, and so we often talk of imaginative and pretend (not real) play.

The ability to adapt in a changing world requires flexibility, openness and an ability to respond creatively to new ideas, feelings, relationships, situations and physical circumstances. These qualities demonstrate intelligence. Human beings are probably the most adaptive animals and play helps children to be flexible thinkers.

Key message

To summarise, children play because it helps them to:
* become symbol users and makers
* develop abstract thought (and so transform their experiences)
* understand other people's ideas, feelings and relationships
* imagine alternative worlds and ways of doing things
* create these in play scenarios
* stay flexible and so develop their intelligence.

You may like to look back to the end of Chapter 1 for an explanation of some terms.

Why do humans have a long childhood?

Flexible thinking and intelligence

A lengthy childhood full of play keeps thinking flexible and helps intelligence to grow.

Human beings have a long childhood so that they stay flexible and delay acting in narrow ways. Other animals do not have the possibility to delay inflexible thinking or feelings and so do not, through having a long childhood, develop richly in their ability to use symbols. Neither do they continue to grow in intelligence. They are, quite literally, stuck in their ways for the whole of their adult lives.

A blackbird can sing only a limited set of tunes. Its alarm call does not vary. The blackbird's mating dance follows a set formula. These behaviours are inflexible. This means a blackbird does not need a long childhood in which to learn these things. These patterns of symbolic behaviour are innate. However, they are triggered into action through experience with other birds. Variations among the song of blackbirds living in different parts of the UK are very slight.

The impact of living with other people, and experience of life, causes physical changes in the brain of a human child across the years of childhood and even into adulthood. So, the human brain keeps changing because of the people we meet and the experiences we have with them (Damasio, 2004). Human babies have the potential to use a wide range of symbols and display symbolic behaviour by the time they are toddlers. During toddler times, human children typically explode into using language (spoken and signed), dance, arts, music, drama, literature, science, and mathematical and logical forms of symbolic behaviour. During this period, their free-flow play has the potential to develop rapidly.

The development of language and play

How babies and toddlers become 'citizens of the world'

Free-flow play (Bruce, 1991, 2010a) opens up rich opportunities for symbolic behaviour during the toddler period. According to Gopnik *et al.* (1999), the development of spoken or signed language is becoming established or is being hardwired into the brain as a universal and cross-cultural symbolic behaviour. But is symbolic, free-flow play also a cross-cultural behaviour?

It is more difficult to study free-flow play than language development, but it too is likely to be hardwired into the brain. To compound the problem, there are huge variations in the way that this process is triggered into action. However, just because something is difficult to study doesn't make it less important.

Gopnik *et al.* (1999) suggest that all human children (unless there is a disability, or delay in development), no matter where they are in the world, are born with the potential in their brains to:

* study and remember faces
* turn facial expressions into feelings
* learn how objects move
* work out how objects disappear
* link cause and effect
* work out how to categorise objects
* work out how the sounds of language divide
* link information from the different senses by forming images
* transform two-dimensional pictures into three-dimensional objects.

These researchers, however, do not focus on whether play is something all human children have the possibility of developing (providing this is triggered by their experiences with other people, and objects). But they do explore the way babies learn spoken or signed languages. There may well be some resonances here which help us to link what is known about language development with what is also likely to happen in the development of free-flow play.

They suggest (Gopnik *et al.*, 1999) that babies are 'citizens of the world'. This means that babies all over the world are capable of becoming speakers and listeners. Language use is one kind of symbol use. However, they point out that, as babies grow up in their particular culture, with a particular group of people, they also become 'culture-bound specialists' (Gopnik *et al.*, 1999). The way play is encouraged or constrained in a particular family or culture will influence the development of the child.

Babies can learn only the spoken languages they hear. They can play only in the ways people show them. Experience influences the forms that language or play will take. Hearing babies usually learn to speak a spoken language, unless, for example, they are growing up in a community of profoundly deaf people where sign language is the norm. In this case, they will learn to sign, using gesture and finger movements and facial expression. Babies in the USA tend to play with adults (Rogoff *et al.*, 1998), whereas babies in Borneo learn about play through other children.

During childhood the brain can easily develop spoken or signed language, or both. After a decade, the window of opportunity for the development of language (spoken or signed) begins to shut. But it doesn't slam, it closes gradually (Blakemore, 2001).

The fact is that some children, by the age of six, can speak and understand several languages and, although it is unusual, can also use sign language fluently. Such children are said to be multilingual.

To be multilingual is to be a proficient and flexible symbol user. It means the child, who has developed a mother tongue and is fluent in other languages, is already rich in symbolic behaviour. Play helps children to try out the spoken or signed languages they learn.

Language, play and culture are closely linked

Children participate in their cultures because to speak a language fluently involves learning the cultural aspects in which the language is rooted. For example, Gujarati speakers do not use 'thank you' in the way of English speakers. In Gujarati, this word is used to express deep and sincere gratitude. In English, it is used as an everyday word, for example to thank the bus conductor who gives the ticket in exchange for money. This cultural distinction will show in the child's play and language.

Children who have experienced different cultural conventions are already able to understand how to manipulate different symbols to mean different things, sometimes with sophisticated layers of meaning. Because they know intimately about differing cultural conventions and symbols, they are not destined to be narrow 'culture-bound specialists'.

Play helps children to experiment with language in ways which are not narrowly culture bound. It encourages children to be citizens of the world because it helps them to create a variety of ways of talking and doing things, which they experiment with in their play scenarios.

Carly (five years) made a puppet out of a wooden peg. She wrapped a piece of blue material around the peg and tied it with string. She drew a face on the top of the peg with a felt pen. She was representing Mary in the Christmas story. She then went to the dolls' house, made the character of a mother and played mummies and children, using the dolls in the dolls' house as babies and children. The peg doll became a prop for her play. She talked as if she was each character, out loud to herself. This was play that needs private space and is not to be shared with others.

'Culture-bound specialists'

Children who are monolingual are able to function at high levels symbolically, but only within their own language. Nor do they have the advantage of participating deeply in the different ways that different languages work. Consequently, their lives are inevitably narrower in perspective.

For example, an English-speaking parent might give a drink to a baby, saying, 'Here's your cup.' The emphasis would be on the word 'cup'. A Korean parent is likely to say, 'It's moving in,' stressing the movement of the cup.

To speak both languages means the toddler learns the words to express ideas and feelings about the cup and how it moves, in several different ways. A monolingual child will learn only to talk about the cup, or the movement in one way. The fascinating thing is that all babies, as they turn to toddlers, seem to learn to use words for cups and movements, whatever the language and cultural variations. It is just that some children have more choice, and flexibility.

Developing a system of meaning through play

The important thing seems to be that toddlers, throughout the world, develop a system of meaning which helps them in both language and play. Jean Mandler (1999) suggests they do this in three ways:

1. Through daily living, babies are helped to look at objects by people. They gradually form images of the objects around them, by relating to the people.
2. Babies are also given objects, such as cups, to manipulate and they try to work out the difference between the three-dimensional and the two-dimensional world. This has great variation across cultures.
3. Babies usually crawl and go to fetch objects they want, or they move to join people.

For most babies, it is not necessary to teach them how to look at objects and people, or to manipulate and play with objects – they do this on their own in their play. Through their play, for example, they confirm which objects move on their own. They establish the difference between living animals and inanimate objects, or the difference between dead animals or animals which are asleep, and people. They explore mechanical things. Again, there is enormous cultural variation in this. Toddlers and young children are curious about how to make an object or person move, fall or bounce. They try to put one object inside another. These early experiences exploring the sense, space, movement, images, objects and people open up possibilities for play.

Again, children in different cultural situations will develop different systems of meaning which, as Jean Mandler suggests, lead them into play and other kinds of symbolic behaviour in deeply different ways. The way that Australian Aboriginal children do this will have little in common with the ways that British children do it in their play.

> Malaguzzi (1996), the Italian educator who pioneered the development of the early childhood curriculum in Reggio Emilia, talked about the 'Hundred Languages of Children', which is another way of saying that there are many ways to play. Children pretend play, play in pairs, make constructions with wooden blocks, etc.

Play looks different in different cultural contexts

Different cultures and communities encourage children to play in different ways.

* Adults may or may not join in the play.
* Children may or may not be given toys to play with.
* Children may play in mixed-age groups away from adults.
* They may be expected to grow out of play by five years, or in middle childhood (by nine years or so).
* Rich childhood play may be linked with adult creativity and imagination.

Cultural contexts in this book

Children growing up in the UK today are growing up in a multicultural world. They often speak more than one language. The children we follow in Part 2 of this book live in an urban context in one of the biggest cities in the world. We shall see how they are learning to play and become symbol users in rich and varied ways.

These children have some things in common:

* They are all human.
* They all live in an urban context.
* They will all learn to speak English.
* They will all attend some kind of early childhood education or care group provision.
* In the group they attend, adults will encourage them to play.

There will be major differences in the lives of these children:

* Some will speak English as an additional language.
* Some will be only children and play alone at home.
* Some will play with adults at home, some will not.

If there are such variations within a group of children growing up in the same city, it doesn't take much to imagine how there will be far-reaching differences in the play of children growing up in different parts of the world.

Principles of equality and inclusion in play

Disability

For some children, play is a challenge. Play, even of a basic kind, may be slow to develop, or the play may remain in an emergent form. Very often, sensitive awareness by people and the careful introduction of objects, music and movement can open up the play, even when such development seemed unlikely. It is of central importance that adults working with children with multi disabilities and complex needs rise to such challenges.

An inclusive approach to play means that there must be great emphasis on creating an environment which encourages play and which provides access to play for children who need special help. Robert Orr (2003) stresses the need to consider access for children who are wheelchair users.

The Danish educator, Lilli Nielsen (1992), believes that all children should have the right to be in a 'den', which is something most children enjoy making for themselves – under tables, or under trees or bushes. She has developed this through making a 'Little Room' for children who have multi disabilities. The adult observes the child to see what interests and engages them, and then makes a den (Little Room) around the child, based on observations.

> The child experiences his (her) world by means of all sensory modalities: he/she experiments with the world, explores it and creates worlds that are his/her own. Through all this he/she achieves the perception of being a part of the surrounding world, and as being separated from objects and persons in this world – as a self.
>
> (Nielsen, 1992)

Gender

Children who move beyond basic play into free-flow play develop the possibility to broaden their view of people. We saw in the Introduction how free-flow play facilitates understanding of the way people from different families and cultures think. It is the features relating to role play, rehearsal for adult life and pretend which contribute to this.

Adults have a tendency to accept the world as it is. They say this is being realistic. The problem is that in doing this, they constrain children's play. Free-flowing play has the possibility to broaden a child's view of other people. Play is partly about helping children to live in a real world, but it is also about how things might be, for better or worse.

Adults need to help children consider life from the point of view of different genders, and to be aware of and respect differences. For example, boys can be pregnant and give birth during play (BBC Radio 4, 1999).

Boys often need support in order to move into role play. Action research by Penny Holland (2003), in her work setting, suggests that the three- and four-year-old boys needed help from an adult to move from posturing with weapons and hero costumes into play scenarios with fuller characterisations and stories that broadened their play. Her research cannot be generalised, but it raises interesting questions to explore.

What do children play at?

* Children at play can create new worlds.
* They experiment with worlds that are better than those that exist in their experience.
* They experiment with worlds full of evil.
* They develop strategies to create good and evil.
* They make stories and characters in their play scenarios which lead into complex areas of later study and interest.
   * Adult literature – drama, poetry and prose.
   * Study of people, past, present and future – evolution, archaeology, history, political theory, geography.
* They make places into new and alternative worlds.
   * They create work environments – shops, factories, markets, farms, hospitals.
   * They make beautiful places – seashore scenes, fairylands, palaces.
   * They make adventures – in deserts, under the sea, in outer space, on holiday.
   * They make dangerous and safe places – with goodies, baddies, families, friends, monsters, superheroes and heroines.

Key message

To summarise, children play because it helps them to:
* become symbol users
* develop abstract thought
* understand other people's ideas, feelings and relationships
* imagine alternative worlds and ways of doing things
* create these in play scenarios
* stay flexible and so develop their intelligence.

Making play fair

Fair play in early childhood practice means that we need to encourage children to:

* become more creative and flexible than they would otherwise be
* be more spiritually aware (knowing and relating to the self, others and the universe)
* be able to experience fully through the arts (such as drama, paintings, sculpture, dance, music, etc.) both humorous and cathartic moments that make life more bearable and manageable.

Summary

Fair play for children does not mean that all children have to play in the same way, wherever they live in the world. What is right for one family, culture or society may not be right for another. The promotion of fair play for children means that we need to embrace differences in childhood play in an inclusive way. We need to provide access to play for children with special educational needs and disabilities, and to consider that boys are not girls and girls are not boys.

REFLECTIVE QUESTIONS FOR YOUR PRACTICE

Observe a child/children at play. Is the play anchored in the here and now, or does the play involve the child or children in using their experiences?

Observe a child/children at play. Do you see children thinking about possible, imaginative situations and scenarios in their play? If so, in what ways? Is this the same for babies, toddlers or children from three to seven years of age?

3 Observing and describing play (babies)

Theory and practice should feed each other

We can make all the theories in the world about play, but a theory is no use at all if it doesn't help us in practice. We need working theories.

Why do we need theories?

Theories help us to predict and anticipate how children might behave and react. They help us to structure what we observe. Theories help us to make sense of what we see. This means that we need to begin by observing (gathering the data which helps us to build theory).

However, we need to be careful not to use theories which narrow down our thinking about childhood play. We want theories which open up our thinking and which challenge what we thought we knew. This will help us to develop our understanding of childhood play.

> ### Key message
> Theories help us to:
> * observe children (and/or adults) at play
> * describe children (and/or adults) at play
> * analyse and make sense of what we see.

When we analyse play, we find ourselves linking what we have found with what other people (pioneers and theorists in Chapter 2) have found. We may find our observations fit with theories or what the pioneers said. We may find they do not. This will help us to think deeply about play, and to keep exploring and finding out more about childhood play. It helps us to see whether we agree or disagree with a particular theory or approach of a pioneer.

The Nobel prize-winning scientist Richard Feynman said:

> The thing that doesn't fit is the most interesting.

Observing babies

Observing the baby's play using narrative observation techniques

There are many different observation techniques – different techniques are useful for different situations and purposes. It is important to find ways of observing which are appropriate to studying play. Some techniques are too simplistic for looking at a complex area such as childhood play.

Traditional narrative observation is recommended for observing and describing children and/or adults at play. This approach, which has stood the test of time, allows rich opportunities for analysing the play afterwards. It is as useful now as it was when it was first developed by Susan Isaacs (see Chapter 2) in the 1930s.

The four steps of narrative observation

1. The observer writes briefly about the context of the observation.
2. The observer writes down as exact a description as possible of what the child says and does. If other children are also involved, the observer writes down enough description of the conversations and actions of other children to give a clear picture of the target child.
3. The observation can then be analysed and interpreted.
4. The observation can be linked with the observations of this child made by other people. It can also be linked with theories to see whether it fits or challenges research findings.

This approach to observation is useful for the following reasons:

* It discourages the observer from making value-laden judgements about families and children.
* It challenges the observer to reflect on cultural differences and to respect families and children, and to take an inclusive approach to special educational needs and disability.
* The observer does not spoil the observation by analysing throughout, because the analysis comes as a later step, after gathering the on-the-spot description.
* The description gives enough detail for the observer to be able to analyse later, without making wild claims that are unsupported by evidence.
* The observation can be given a particular focus for analysis. In this book, the focus when analysing observations will be on childhood play.
* The analysis deepens when the observer makes use of current theory and research to support and illuminate the interpretation made.

It is important when observing only to describe what the child is doing or saying. An adult who starts interpreting while observing will spoil the observation, perhaps becoming distracted or, more seriously, seeing only those features of play which fit a particular theory.

The **narrative observation form** in this chapter shows the different elements of a narrative observation. This form can be used when observing babies or children. Some people like to write their observations on a form like this. Others prefer to note the headings, but to write about them on a plain piece of paper, which doesn't look like a form.

Photographs are very useful in enhancing narrative observations. They can highlight some of the important moments. Written permission must be granted by parents. It is now common practice for this to be discussed in the first meeting with parents, so that they are reassured that photographs will not be shared beyond the specific purpose of the child's record (often called the learning journey). Every setting now needs a policy on photography which addresses issues of child protection, so that parents feel secure about the way photographs are used.

The same requirements apply for video recording, which is an invaluable modern tool for narrative observation. If Susan Isaacs had been alive today, she would surely have made use of photography and video as a rich description of exactly what happened. The advantage is that the video recording can be replayed again and again. Each time it is viewed, fascinating new observations are made and the analysis can be deepened. Video analysis seems to open up the possibility of adding layer upon layer of meaning and insight to the observation.

Figure 3.1: In this photograph, each baby is responding in a different way, right from the start, and is being encouraged to do so. They might want to stand; have their dummy before they relax into the session; lie on their back, gazing at their mother; sit on their mother's lap; be held around the middle by their mother. Every baby is unique.

However, it must be used with care and sensitivity as it can make some children feel self-conscious if they are not familiar with it. Once it becomes established, though, children take little notice of it (Athey, 1990).

The narrative observation gives an exact description of what has happened, and the communication that has taken place. This might take the form of eye contact between a baby or child and adults. You might note the tone of voice used, or some other form of non-verbal communication with the baby or child. Non-verbal communication is important throughout life, and spoken language emerges out of it.

Narrative observation

Child's name ....

Date of observation ....

Time observation begins ....

Time observation ends ....

Short description of context in which the observation is being made

....

....

....

Description of what is happening ....

....

....

....

Communication (both non-verbal and spoken) ....

....

With self ....

With others ....

Adapted from Bartholomew and Bruce (1994)

Working through an observation

What is the cultural and community context?

Different cultures and communities in different parts of the world encourage baby massage. Baby massage is a time-honoured tradition in India, for example. It relaxes babies and increases their physical and emotional well-being. It also strengthens the bonding and attachment between baby and mother, father or carer. From the point of view of this book, it has another advantage: it supports play. Over the past 30 years it has become established practice in some parts of the UK, although it is embraced more in some communities than others.

In the photographs in this chapter, the mothers are led by an adult who is trained in baby massage. This is often a health visitor, nurse, or Level 3 practitioner. It is clear from looking at the photographs that both babies and mothers are enjoying this session. They meet regularly. The leader explains that it doesn't matter if the baby is tired, not in the mood, needs changing or feeding, and so does not join in. Pressure to conform would spoil and undermine the point of baby massage.

In the group, one baby needed changing, one needed feeding, and one was asleep and never woke up in time. This is only the second session – most mothers are still feeling they are beginner learners, and are not yet confident and experienced. They need plenty of help from the leader to be relaxed themselves and to open up their own enjoyment, so that they create an atmosphere which encourages their baby to relax and begin to enjoy the situation, and to wallow in their play.

Describing the physical context

The walls are not 'busy'. Some rooms have so many things on the walls and even the windows that they make it impossible to be calm and relax. Busy walls and windows can over-stimulate and be unpleasant, with vibrant colours and every space infilled. These walls are plain; the curtains are a soft neutral colour; the floor is a quiet colour and so are the chair covers.

This means that babies and mothers can concentrate on each other and on the feel of the oil on the skin, and the relaxing movements of the massage. The arms relax, the hands uncurl, the feet become floppy as the thighs and legs are massaged. It is as if the massage rituals cause a falling away of tension, so that baby and mother are opening up a calm space for play. This is play that involves the developing sense of identity of the baby – who am I? I am me, and you are separate.

It takes about three years for this process to complete, and here are the beginnings. Massage offers the opportunity for baby and mother to get to know each other, and for babies to work out with increasing understanding where they begin and end, and all about their physical selves and their identity.

Gathering observations through description

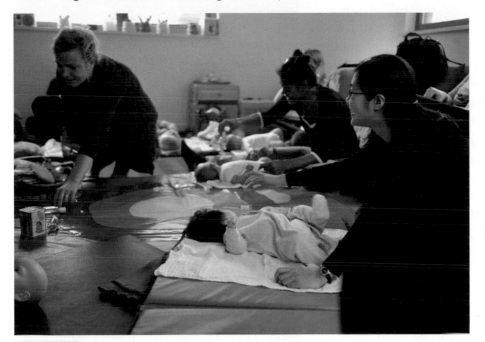

Figure 3.2: The babies are placed on their back, and they turn to their side when their mothers show them the bottle of oil.

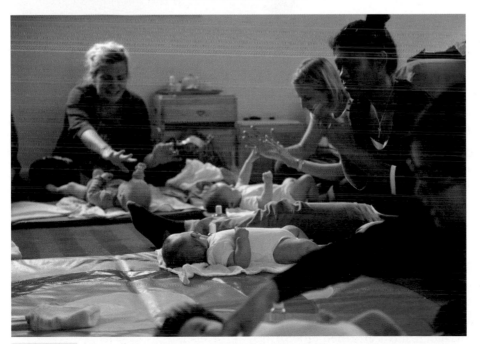

Figure 3.3: The mothers talk to their babies and show them their hands covered in oil. Slow and gentle introduction to each stage of the massage process is important, as babies become anxious if things are suddenly presented and rushed upon them.

Babies vary in the positions they move into. In fact, it is a sign of success when babies move to be comfortable and enjoy the massage fully. The leader talks the mothers gently through the process, using a doll to demonstrate. Gradually, mothers begin to follow her lead. Each baby begins to show their personal style and response by showing initiative, and leading the mother as much as she leads the baby. It becomes a two–way communication.

Figure 3.4: At first, the fists are tight and the baby is still – he/she is adjusting to the feelings of the massage and thinking about it.

Communication (both non-verbal and spoken)

As the mothers become more relaxed, they focus less on the leader demonstrating and more on their baby. This means they begin to pick up on what their babies 'say' to them. Babies may not be able to use words to say things, but they have a great deal to say in the form of non-verbal communication. They draw their mothers to them through the way they look into their eyes. They move their arms and legs so that their mother massages them as a reply and mutters nonsense things to them in baby talk (which Trevarthen (1998) calls 'motherese'). The mothers use their own languages to do this, as several languages, together with English, are spoken in the group. The mother and baby are performing a dance and song together, completely tuned into each other. They begin to play in dance and song form. (Malloch and Trevarthen (2008))

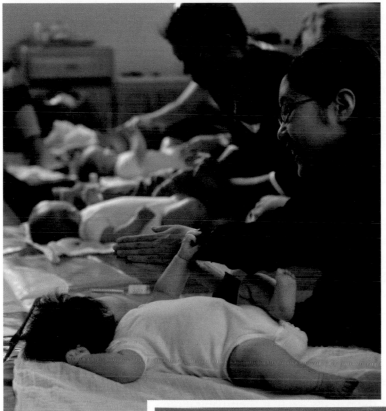

Figure 3.5: The babies begin to relax – their hands unfurl and their feet go floppy. Their mothers relax with them. The mother focuses on the baby and does not look around so much; the baby begins to lead the mother. This relaxed situation opens up a place for play.

Interpreting and analysing observations

Be aware of your own theories

Everyone has personal theories which guide them through their lives. However, not many people are aware of having them. Some people believe that they are objective thinkers, but this is not humanly possible.

It would be a very boring and machine-like world if people didn't have personal theories about life. The important thing is to be aware that we have them, even though we don't necessarily know what they are! This is particularly important when studying play.

We noted in Chapters 1 and 2 that play varies in different parts of the world, in different cultures and in different families. It is a certainty that each one of us will have a personal theory about childhood play. This will be influenced by our upbringing, our cultural context and where we live in the world.

So, we need to be aware that we may have a narrow, monocultural view of play. One of the main reasons for undertaking narrative observations is to find a way of opening up our thinking to encompass a broader view of play. Then we can help children and families to get the most out of their learning in ways which are right for them.

Parental expertise

It is important that the parents see that their baby enjoys the massage session, and under the skilled care of the leader, this is achieved. However, most parents will probably not realise that their interactions lead them into a situation of free-flowing play. It is never a good idea to become analytical during moments of play. What matters is to experience the richness and deepness of play. Then it can be discussed later.

Quite a number of adults have not experienced rich moments of play and may have engaged only fleetingly in play of superficial kinds in their own childhoods. Sessions like this open up the possibilities for parents to learn about play with and through their children. They are able to understand play only if they recognise its powerful possibilities for their child's development of relationships with people, feelings and ideas, through their physical, moving bodies.

The approach of the pioneers of the early childhood curriculum

It is fascinating to look at the writings of some of the pioneers of early childhood education and care in the Western world, to see what they say about play (Bruce, 2004, 2011b; Bruce *et al.*, 2010b). There is more about these in Chapter 2. There are some recurring themes in their views, including features of play, which seem to link with what modern researchers think is important about play.

Treasure basket play for sitting babies

It would be interesting to see whether observation of the sitting baby in Figure 3.6, playing with the treasure basket, leads to the identification of any features of play. Treasure baskets were the pioneering idea of Elinor Goldschmied (see Forbes, 2004), who advocated the use of natural materials. The basket is carefully designed for sitting babies, so that if the baby leans on the rim with a hand or arm and reaches into the basket to grasp an object with the other hand, the basket will not tip over. Three babies can share a basket and the contents of baskets can be themed to give a broad range of sensual experiences. It is important not to put anything into the basket that you don't feel comfortable about.

In this basket the baby selects and spends most time with a ribbon and pastry brush, with a passing interest in a piece of shiny wrapping material.

Key message
The 12 features of play

1. In their play, children use the first-hand experiences that they have in life.
2. Children make up rules as they play and so keep control of their play.
3. Children make play props.
4. Children choose to play. They cannot be made to play.
5. Children rehearse the future in their role play.
6. Children pretend when they play.
7. Children play alone sometimes.
8. Children and/or adults play together, in parallel, associatively, or cooperatively in pairs or groups.
9. Each player has a personal play agenda, although they may not be aware of this.
10. Children playing will be deeply involved and difficult to distract from their deep learning. Children at play wallow in their learning.
11. Children try out their most recent learning, skills and competencies when they play. They seem to celebrate what they know.
12. Children at play coordinate their ideas, feelings and make sense of relationships with their family, friends and culture. When play is coordinated it flows along in a sustained way. It is called free-flow play.

Developed from Bruce (1991, 1996)

Figure 3.6: In this sequence of photographs, we can see that the baby is a stable sitter and can twist and turn without toppling every time. At first the baby chooses to explore a ribbon. Concentration on this continues for some time. Then the baby switches to holding the pastry brush, turning it this way and that. The baby seems to be comparing the ribbon and the stick. They are both trajectories. (To find out more about schemas, see Bruce 2011b, or Bruce *et al.*, 2010b.) One is a soft trajectory and its shape changes as it is touched; the other is a solid wooden trajectory and does not change.

Using the 12 features of play in the analysis

* The baby is using his senses. At the moment, he is gaining the first-hand experiences which he will later use in his play. (This links with feature 1.)
* He already chooses when to play and when he is not in the mood for it. His key person in the nursery is learning when he will enjoy playing and when it is not a good time. (Feature 4)
* He is happily playing alone, although his key person is sitting near him, ready to help when needed and interested in his play without interfering in it. Babies always need companionship and should not be left alone or they become lonely. That is different from enjoying their own company in the presence of others. (Feature 7)
* In this observation, it is evident that he likes to play with adults, especially those he knows. (Feature 8). Babies this young can play together with a treasure basket, but in this case the baby is alone.
* He has his own play agenda. (Feature 9). He is exploring two different kinds of trajectory: pliable (the flowing nature of the ribbon) and rigid (the handle of the pastry brush).
* He wallows in his playing, giving it his all. (Feature 10)
* He is already showing off his latest skills in his play. (Feature 11). He is concentrating with more and more depth, twisting and turning objects with his wrist and his body in order to see them from all angles and seek out their properties.
* His play coordinates his learning. He is using what he knows about. (Feature 12)

It is quite amazing to see how many of the features of free flow play are already in evidence. Seven out of the twelve seem to be present in this play scenario.

One feature we did not see was playing with another baby, or his key person, but that is because he is the only baby at the treasure basket. The features which have yet to emerge are, unsurprisingly, those which deal with the imaginative and creative (symbolic) aspects of play, for example, rehearsal of roles, or pretending, making and using play props, or drawing on experience to make a play scenario. Some of the first play of this kind is, all over the world, food preparation play. Two- and three-year-olds often play at making meals, and cooking and shopping.

This baby is well on the way to free-flow play in all its aspects.

Using what modern experts say in the analysis

Penelope Leach (1997) says:

> Although newborn babies cannot handle toys or take part in games, even the youngest of them can certainly get bored and lonely.

Babies enjoy looking at objects hanging from a play frame. Leach points out that although babies cannot tell us what they like, we know they look for longer at things they prefer. Babies often like to gaze at the light in the ceiling, to look into the eyes of either parent, to look at hanging objects and other items.

The hanging objects need to be at a perfect focusing distance of 20–25 cm (8–10 inches) from the bridge of the baby's nose. This is also the distance at which we naturally hold the baby in our arms to talk to her. The light is further away but, although a blur, it can be seen – it is of interest. Babies are biologically predisposed to prefer objects near to them, if given the choice. This encourages them to focus on people, to make relationships, to talk and play with others. Leach (1997) points out:

> If, armed with this information, you deliberately put things close enough to your baby's eyes for him to see them clearly, he will 'choose' to pay attention to much more subtle stimuli than brightness or movement.

Babies prefer their mother's or father's voice to that of a stranger. Leach (1997) says:

> Unless you are on the look-out for it, you may not notice how much your baby enjoys your voice during these first weeks . . . he often listens to your voice without looking at you . . . When you begin to speak to him, he will start to move excitedly.

Babies hold their hands in a tight fist. If we were to put something in the palm, the baby would hold it tightly in a reflex grasp. But babies cannot yet release at will an object they are holding. At about three months of age, babies begin to use rattles to hold.

Parents often talk to their babies about the movement and direction of the toy. They say things like, 'It's coming over.' Someone with English as their first language would be more likely to say, 'Do you want this? It's round.'

Different languages emphasise different things. Research (Talmy, 1999) suggests that all children all over the world, although their parents emphasise different things (e.g. The line of movement of an object, or the object itself), by the time they themselves begin to speak seem to know about objects and the movements they make.

It is also interesting that parents speak to their babies in motherese and fatherese. Colwyn Trevarthen (1998) calls this kind of talking to babies in a high tone a proto-conversation – the person speaking to the baby, as well as speaking in a high voice, also speaks slowly and emphasises important words. This is, in fact, an early sort of conversation, without words. It involves a lot of moving together, almost as if the adult and baby are in a partner dance using sound. This is the beginning of language, but it is also the beginning of dance, music and poetry. This kind of play lays the foundations for learning later on.

Through their play, babies learn the crucial things which will help them to create a system of meaning that they will develop throughout their lives through:

* looking at people's faces and forming images
* encountering objects and learning how to touch them and interact with them
* listening and moving to the voices of people they love and feeling their movement in tune with theirs.

Summary

Perhaps it is a good thing we are not aware that the play we enjoy with babies is such an education for them, or we might spoil the pleasure of it. As soon as we get serious about it, we ruin the educational benefit. As we learn more and more about human development, we must be careful not to damage the learning through play that babies engage in so energetically. This seems to be a problem in some parts of the world. Parents in the UK are very vulnerable to these pressures at this time in history.

We must remember there is now overwhelming evidence that babies need other people to activate (neuroscientists use the word 'trigger') and empower their natural learning. This does not mean that they need other people to control their learning, for in doing so adults will constrain it.

In this chapter, we have seen how a baby massage session helped mothers to really interact with their babies, so that their babies were opened up to play and the babies began to lead the adults as much as the adults led the babies. Children who do not learn to play are constrained in their learning.

In this book, the emphasis is on encouraging adults to develop their observation skills, so that they can analyse and interpret play using the heritage of the early pioneers, together with current research and theory. Then adults can help children to do their own learning through play.

REFLECTIVE QUESTIONS FOR YOUR PRACTICE

Explore mobiles and observe babies using them. The distance of the mobile from the baby's eyes is of central importance.

Observe the way babies in the first six months use their hands in relation to objects. Can you predict when the baby is ready to play with rattles and hold objects?

Find out the exact measurements for a treasure basket as designed by Elinor Goldschmied. These are necessary because they allow sitting babies to reach into the basket without frustration. Make sure there is a rim on which the baby can lean without the basket tipping up.

Observe babies using treasure baskets. The quality of the play is greater if the correct design of basket is used.

4 How play makes sense of learning

Human beings have a long childhood

As we saw in Chapter 2, human beings have a very long childhood compared with other mammals. Going to school is part of the learning that takes place during childhood for some children, although not all children in the world go to school – many will be beginning work by the age of seven or eight. Even so, compared with a chimpanzee, a childhood of seven or eight years is still a long time.

Why do humans have a long childhood?

We have a comparatively long childhood for a variety of reasons.

* It encourages flexible thinking.
* Flexible thinking allows intelligence to grow.
* It allows experimentation with feelings.
* It helps children to get their feelings under control.
* It allows children to get inside someone else's mind, while remaining themselves (decentration or theory of mind).
* It encourages awareness, sensitivity, empathy and understanding of others, which helps good relationships to develop.
* It encourages children to reflect, through the appropriate process of play, on moral issues such as goodness and evil, fairness and justice.
* It gives them opportunities to learn about their culture.
* It gives children time to play.

Children do not play unless the process is 'triggered' by people, but they are biologically predisposed to play. So, we can say there are biological and socio-cultural aspects to play development.

Children are born with a physical brain that is genetically set to develop in ways particular to being a human. But each child's brain is also a unique brain, which is different from anyone else's. Examples of the biological aspects of development are that the child, unless there is a disability or some other constraint, will learn to sit, crawl, walk, talk and play.

These biologically driven processes need to be triggered by other people. A baby is helpless without other people. If a baby is never spoken to or played with, that baby does not develop language or play. It is more obvious if language does not develop than if the development of play is absent.

Key message

Both the biological and socio-cultural aspects of development are important in the development of play.

As we observed in Chapter 3, babies learn to play with their families and key people they know well and spend time with. Both the biological and socio-cultural aspects of babies' lives are important.

Observing toddlers' play

Toddlers also spend a great deal of time relating to people, exploring their own cultural and physical context, and trying to make sense of their lives through their play. But they have become mobile and can stand up and walk about, which gives them more choice and independence. Independence is exciting for toddlers to experience, but it also becomes overwhelming for them at times and so they need to be with sensitive adults who understand this.

In most parts of the world, adults are not aware that the child is learning so much through their play. However, cross-cultural studies (Whiting and Edwards, 1992) indicate that children in nomadic, agricultural settled or post-industrial lifestyles all, in one way or another, seem to benefit from having space and time to play.

Some toddlers learn about play with adults. This is particularly so in the Western world of Europe and the USA. Others play mainly with older siblings (brothers and sisters). Of course, play will be different in form depending on the way the child is initiated in it (Rogoff *et al.*, 1998).

Heuristic play

Elinor Goldschmied developed heuristic play for toddlers. The idea is that the children are offered, in a group, different objects and containers which they can play with without adult intervention. They play for a certain time, and not in the main area but away from all the other experiences on offer, so that the focus is on the heuristic play context (Forbes, 2004). Children who are just beginning to walk love to tip things out and put things in, and this kind of play satisfies this biological need.

Objects which might be placed in the sacks and hung on the wall at the end of the session are, for example, containers which are large tins and cardboard boxes, cardboard tubes of various sizes, shallow containers and snack boxes, small baskets, tree mugs and kitchen roll holders, knitting cones. Then there need to be objects that can be put into these containers, such as corks, furniture knobs, shells, cotton reels, lids of various sorts, etc.

Heuristic play allows children to explore and to find out how different objects behave. There should be plenty of objects so that in a group every child has enough to explore. Otherwise quarrels will break out.

The objects should be set out around the space and the children brought into the area. The children sense that this is going to be new and exciting to explore. They need plenty of time to find out what is on offer before they are ready to play. Some children seek out things which are similar, some put things in and out of containers. Every child has their own play agenda and play style as part of that.

The session should last for as long as the children's interest lasts – it is not unusual for children to concentrate for an hour or near. Ideally, the children will help the adult to put the objects away into the sack at the end of the session. Toddlers love to help the adult hang the sacks of objects on pegs on the wall ready for the next session.

Although toddlers growing up in the UK are often given toys, they also enjoy the cross-cultural and time-honoured play indulged in by toddlers all over the world which heuristic play builds on.

When they are not sure about what they are about to do (which is often!), toddlers typically look back at their parent or key person to check their reaction. Judy Dunn (1991) calls this 'affective tuning'. For example, they might clamber on and off a chair if a chair is there, but if not, they will apply the same treatment to a person!

If they feel secure enough, toddlers will frequently leave a loved person they are playing with to fetch an object and bring it back to them. They often make a move to get to know a newcomer by offering them an object, although they usually take it back immediately!

They show people things, as if to develop a conversation through their play. They seem to 'ask' to hold objects by stretching out their arms and holding their hands open. They might make word-like sounds as they do so.

Linking the observation to theory

In Chapter 3, we saw that the babies are already demonstrating rich play. The play develops in complexity during the toddler period and we see that play with objects and people moves into pretend play – the child is becoming an emergent symbol user and symbol maker.

It takes time – two or three years – to develop enough first-hand experience of living to be able to turn the experiences into play. Toddlers need to manipulate, discover and explore, using their senses and movement of their increasingly coordinated bodies.

Jean Mandler (1999) suggests that toddlers are developing a system of meaning that will lead them into increasingly complex layerings in their play.

They can move about freely once they can walk. Being mobile means toddlers can go and fetch objects, or show people things that interest them by taking them to them or calling them over to see. Being able to walk gives more control over life, but it is also a little scary to be so free. Toddlers need constant reassurance by having people they love near them. This gives them the confidence to have independent adventures on the other side of the room, or even out of view.

Figure 4.1: She crawls over to her key person.

Figure 4.2: She rises to indicate to her that she wants to walk.

Figure 4.3: She claps her hands to show she is pleased her key person is cooperating.

Figure 4.4: She looks at her hands and at her key person's hands (who clapped her hands in response to her).

Figure 4.5: She takes a few steps of solo wobbly walking, then sinks to the ground and sits for a bit, looking around at the other children in the garden.

Figure 4.6: She crawls again to her key person and repeats the request to be helped up. This time she chooses not to walk alone but to hold her hand and walk with her. Walking is a tiring business.

Key message
The 12 features of play

1. Using first-hand experiences.
2. Making up rules.
3. Making props.
4. Choosing to play.
5. Rehearsing the future.
6. Pretending.
7. Playing alone.
8. Playing together.
9. Having a personal agenda.
10. Being deeply involved.
11. Trying out recent learning.
12. Coordinating ideas, feelings and relationships for free-flow play.

(Adapted from Bruce 1991, 1996)

Using the 12 features of play in the analysis

* These kinds of first-hand experiences (crawling and walking) involve her in using all the senses, as she touches different surfaces in the garden, enjoys outdoor smells and tastes in the air, sees different looks of bushes and clouds in the sky, and hears different sounds as she listens and moves. (Feature 1)

* She has made a little sequence of crawling to her key person and reaching out for her hand to steady her and help her along. This is repeated over and over again. It is her own little rule, which she applies as she plays. (Feature 2)

* She is not yet making her own play props, but she is finding and using props from her environment for her play. She uses her key person as a play prop (something toddlers do a great deal) and also at different points she uses the large and small teddies, the wooden toy and other objects provided in the nursery.

  In this, she is like children all over the world. She makes use of what she can find and turns them into play props. She has a lot more freedom to do this than the baby in Chapter 3. She can walk to fetch and carry objects she wants. She can walk over to a person she wants to be near, or away from them if she wishes. She can hold objects in her hands, but she can do more than the baby in that she can open and close her hands. This means she can choose to pick something up – she doesn't have to wait for something to be put in her hand for her to grasp. She can also drop or release an object from her grip. This allows her to play in a variety of ways with objects. (Feature 3)

* She cannot be made to play. Anyone who tries to make a toddler do something they do not want to do will have difficulty. However, because, as

Judy Dunn (1988) says, toddlers are affectively tuned, they are very interested in what other people who are important to them are doing. Providing, like the baby, the toddler is not tired, uncomfortable or hungry, he or she is likely to be interested in what the people around are doing.

There is a difference between copying and imitating what others do. Copying is doing passively exactly what the other person does; imitating means taking the idea and transforming it into your own. By imitating, the toddler is able to reconstruct a situation in a way that makes meaning for her. We catch a glimpse of this in her play with walking. She has experience of seeing people walk. She chooses to do so at one point in her play, but not for long. She is imitating this movement and turning it into a play sequence. If we tried to make her walk, she would probably refuse! Children need to choose when and what to play.

Children who, from an early age, choose their play do not remain totally dependent on adults in their play. They begin to lead their play and to structure it for themselves. Such children are more likely to become creative thinkers as adults. (Feature 4)

* This little girl is not yet involved in role play as she walks. It contains the seed of it, though. It is not far to walk like someone you see walking, such as the police officer or shopper. (Feature 5)
* The toddler doesn't yet pretend a play scenario with a story and characters. This possibility will come later. (Feature 6)
* She does play alone, but usually in the company of her mother or other members of the family, or within a friendship group. To be entirely alone at play, she would need to feel very secure. Toddlers soon need company. In evolutionary terms, this is probably because they would be in danger if they went off alone. All young mammals need to stay with adults until they know enough to be safe alone. (Feature 7)
* She can play in parallel with other children, but there aren't any present on this occasion who are in the mood or able to help her. Her key person is sensitive to her needs and supports her play alongside her. They cooperate. She can extend her play with someone she is close to, such as her mother or key person, and this is because they are willing to let her lead the play. It will be interesting to see if she becomes a play leader when she widens her circle and begins to play cooperatively with other children. Some children find it difficult to play unless they are the leader all the time. Others like to be followers. Ideally, children will experiment with being both leaders and followers in their play. This will help them to become good team members, but also able to lead. (Feature 8)
* She has a strong play agenda. She wants to walk and celebrate that she can! This links to the next feature, which involves the delight of wallowing in being able to walk without help (but only if you know help is near). (Feature 9)

* She is very involved in her play and cannot be distracted from it. She is wallowing in her play with walking. (Feature 10)

* She is definitely triumphant about her ability to walk. This is a fairly recent piece of learning. It really is as if she needs to show it off. This is a fine example of the joy of learning for young children. Children who are always at the stage of struggling in their learning, and who never become competent enough to gain the mastery they need in order to enjoy what they have learned, will become reluctant learners. For example, there are many children who never enjoy writing stories. They have not had enough experience of creating play scenarios with a storyline (narrative) and characters who have adventures. Children who have not created stories in their play will find it very difficult to write stories later. Because it is very difficult for them to do, they will probably try to avoid it. Famous writers from Western culture who as children created play scenarios of a rich kind include H.G. Wells, the Brontës (Branwell, Charlotte, Emily and Anne) and E.E. Nesbitt. They developed mastery of storytelling in their play, which later turned into creative writing.

This toddler is trying out her latest learning with skill, as she walks around the garden. Providing she walks on even ground, she shows technical prowess in her play. If she is on uneven ground, she is quickly frustrated and overwhelmed. (Feature 11)

* She is coordinating what she knows about walking and bringing together her knowledge in her play. She sits and looks around when she takes a fall, links with her key person to get herself up and to get herself steady, ready to take off on her own. (Feature 12)

Play is a process

This toddler is well on the way to playing using all 12 features of play. It looks as if there is no purpose, product or outcome to what she is doing. But that is the whole point about play: it definitely should not have a purpose, product or outcome.

It cannot be pinned down into a product. It keeps flowing along. It keeps the learning open and flexible. The minute it has a product, it is no longer free-flowing play.

There are many kinds of very valid learning which humans engage in that do have a purpose and a product. For example, learning to cook a cake requires the cook to learn the recipe, or to be able to read it. But this is not play. Children at play are able to stay flexible, respond to events and changing situations, be sensitive to people, adapt, think on their feet, and keep altering what they do in a fast-moving scene.

When the process of play is rich, it can lead children into creating rich products in their stories, paintings, dances, music making, drawings, sculptures and constructions, or in the solving of scientific and mathematical problems.

Sade, four years, played parking the car. She pretended to drive around with a pretend steering wheel and tried to find parking spaces. She parked, looking behind her, and then put money in the parking meter. 'I'm parking my car,' she told an adult.

By the age of five years, James and Caroline can spend an afternoon playing with Action Man and Sindy. They both have their own play ideas, of course, but in cooperative play all the different ideas become involved. The children link and connect their play ideas. They decide that Action Man goes on an expedition and Sindy joins him. They dress her in his clothes because she can't wear high heels on a mountain.

Play helps children make sense of their learning

In short, play helps children to develop their intelligence. William Calvin (1997) says that intelligence is what you use when you don't know what to do.

Children at play don't know what is coming next. They have to work out what to do. A toddler might not know in advance that he would feel unsteady when he stood on the chair. He would have to work out what to do when that happened. Children need to be able to quickly reach for the adult's hand, knowing they are there to help when needed, and balance is difficult. It encourages a 'have a go' attitude.

> ### Key message
> It really does seem to be true to say that children are trying to make sense of their lives when they play.

Summary

Human children are born with the biological possibility to become flexible thinkers and to remain open to learning for the whole of their lives. Play helps intelligence to develop.

Because humans are social animals, babies and toddlers need other people to trigger the biological process of play. Babies and toddlers benefit from play with people and objects. So, the learning through play is both biological and socio-cultural.

Play helps children dare to learn, even when they are uncertain about what will happen. It creates an attitude of mind which is curious, investigative, risk taking and full of adventure.

Play is a process. It cannot be pinned down and made into a product because it needs to flow.

Play makes sense – it helps children to make sense of their lives.

REFLECTIVE QUESTIONS FOR YOUR PRACTICE

Observe a play scenario in which a toddler uses a person or an everyday object, such as a chair, as a play prop. Do toddlers need toys?

Make a collection of containers and objects suitable and safe for heuristic play for a group of eight toddlers. Observe the children at play and act on your observations to improve your collection.

Consider the role of the key person. Are you interpreting this in the way it was conceived and intended? See Elfer, P. And Grenier, J., Chapter 12, in Bruce (2010a).

5 How play helps develop abstract ideas

Moving from the present into the past and future

Play helps children to become abstract thinkers. This means that they do not have to do everything here and now. They can remember back and think forward. Their thinking can be mobile and free flowing. This is why the phrase 'free-flowing play' is so useful: it has in it the essence of what play brings to learning.

We have seen that even babies and toddlers like to play with people and objects. As they become increasingly able to coordinate their bodies, so their play becomes more complex.

Play acts as a navigational tool for young children, making the abstract have form and making the intangibleness of ideas tangible and manageable. It helps children to understand in concrete form all about space, time and reasons why things happen. It helps thinking and ideas to form.

Figure 5.1: The girl is teasing out two aspects of the blocks. They can make long lines and they look different when they stand flat or on their side. She is making what she calls 'a road', with the middle being flat and the sides being upright. Children often give a name to something they build or make at the end of the process. It is only then that their thoughts are put into words.

Figure 5.2 – 5.5: The girls are working side by side in their block play. They don't talk to each other, but they are sensitive to each other, giving each other enough space and each allowing the other to develop their ideas.

> ## Key message
>
> Spoken or signed language helps children to move beyond the here and now into the past and future.

A sense of self

By the age of about two years, children have often become talkers or signers. Communication helps children to explore who they are.

Not only can they sit, crawl and walk, they can also run and jump on two legs together. What they do makes other people react in different ways, so that they can cause anger or laughter, are swept up into someone's arms out of the way of danger, or are cuddled when they are upset.

They are developing a sense of self. This means they are beginning to understand that they are different from other people, with their own unique body, feelings, thoughts and ideas, and friends and loved ones. Understanding other people is another way in which children go beyond themselves into more abstract thinking.

It takes three years or so to work all this out. Moving on from being a toddler is a huge transformation. We can see the scale of change if we study the child's play during this time of transition.

Children develop imagination from images in their minds

Imaginative people can think beyond the way things are. They can transform images into new ideas, feelings and relationships. When they process these images in their brains to make new images, they are imagining.

Babies and toddlers are able to form images. How else could they remember faces?

Images help humans to move from existing entirely in the here and now (the present) into the past and future. It is easier to remember a face you have seen before (in the past) than it is to see a face and then anticipate what the person will do next (in the future).

So, images are central to being able to imagine. Objects can contribute, too. Seeing a spoon helps the baby to anticipate and imagine a mealtime. 'Images' need not be visual – our brains can use sound and smell images to help us move beyond the present. Such images will be central to the imaginations of babies with a visual impairment, for example.

> ## Key message
>
> Developing a sense of 'I', 'me' and 'you' (identity) helps children to understand that what they do influences how things will be in the future.

Being able to imitate others helps children to reconstruct experiences in new ways

Imitation is another important part of the process of moving out of the here and now, and of developing the possibility of thinking about the past or future.

Observing a child imitate

Two-year-olds learn some of the movements for playing with a ball by watching other people. They imitate them.

Successful imitation involves two things:

1. There is the socio-cultural aspect, which influences what and who children imitate.

2. The other aspect of imitation is biological. In order to imitate people she has seen playing football, the child must be sufficiently physically coordinated to throw the ball and catch it. Children can throw the ball better than they can catch it. The more toddlers try to throw and catch, the more practised they will become.

Development and learning through play

Biological influences

The biological possibility to throw and catch a ball is present in young children. However, in order for it to emerge, they need to play with a ball or, even better, to be helped by other people to play with a ball. Biological structures (the ability to throw) are triggered by playing ball with an adult. They then develop increasing skill through experience.

We need to look at the way nature (biological development) and nurture (socio-cultural development) help each other along in a child's development. Through play with objects and people, children gain mastery and strive to develop further.

Biological development enables children to pick up objects and throw them. This isn't as easy as it sounds. Some objects present more challenges than others in this respect. We need to look at what is involved and how childhood play helps the process along.

* Sitting babies tend to be given objects and toys which are easy to hold in one hand, using a palmar grip.
* Crawlers begin to go and get objects they like the look of. The objects are not always easy to grasp or grip. This widens their world and challenges them (and adults living with them!).
* Toddlers love to hold an object in each hand and to walk about with these. They frequently drop them, by accident or on purpose, and put huge effort into picking them up.

❋ Small children, as they turn into steady walkers, love to carry things about. They transport things in their hands, but also in bags, baskets and wheeled vehicles that can be pushed along. They rarely sit still, and nor should they be made to! They cannot learn effectively if they cannot move (Goddard–Blythe, 2000). This is because to sit still requires huge effort for a young child, as they have to coordinate many different parts of their body in order to do so.

Throwing a ball is not as difficult as catching it (Davies, 2003). Children also find it difficult to aim where to throw the ball.

Children frequently use their arms as wings, as if to develop their sense of balance. They are also learning to turn the body rapidly in spins, without falling over.

At first children think in separate images, rooted in the here and now. As thinking becomes more mobile, it transforms images into moving thoughts which will help to consider the past and future with ease. Then they are able to anticipate (think of the future) where the ball will land.

Biologically, children need to practise gripping, releasing, spreading their hands, reaching for objects and working out how to get hold of them when they move. It is difficult to function as an adult without being able to do these things. All of these actions are part of preparing a meal, riding a bike, crossing a road with a pram, doing the shopping, replacing a light bulb.

In their play, children practise these actions in safety

Socio-cultural influences

A child's play is deeply influenced by the socio-cultural aspects of life. For example, the boy in the photograph is attracted to the sunglasses of his key person. He wants to try them on. Sunglasses have become an important item of clothing since greater understanding has developed of the damage of too

Figure 5.6: The boy wants to participate in wearing sunglasses, which he has begun to appreciate is an important item of clothing in his community and culture. Hats, shoes and items such as glasses are often the first dressing-up clothes children choose to wear.

much sunshine and brightness on eyesight, and he has intuitively picked up on this. Children are very good at sensing the importance of objects such as iPods, mobile phones, sunglasses, etc.

Items such as sunglasses are often the first dressing-up clothes children select. They are only one step from reality and the child has not yet moved into being a character. They are still themselves, 'being like' someone else.

> ## Key message
> ### The 12 features of play
>
> 1. Using first-hand experiences.
> 2. Making up rules.
> 3. Making props.
> 4. Choosing to play.
> 5. Rehearsing the future.
> 6. Pretending.
> 7. Playing alone.
> 8. Playing together.
> 9. Having a personal agenda.
> 10. Being deeply involved.
> 11. Trying out recent learning.
> 12. Coordinating ideas, feelings and relationships for free-flow play.
>
> (Adapted from Bruce 1991, 2010a)

This interest in his key person's sunglasses is one of the ways of developing a warm and strong relationship. It is fascinating to see how he finds it difficult to put the sunglasses on himself. This is because, although he has developed the palmar movement in his hands, the pincer movement (coordination of finger and thumb) is still developing. He is not playing with the sunglasses but struggling to put them on.

He is typical of a child at this point in development, in that he doesn't want help – he wants to do it himself, even if he can't! Fortunately, on this occasion all is well and he manages it after a struggle. Children often become very frustrated. They know what they want to do, because they are beginning to be more mobile in their thinking – they can imagine what they want to happen. But their bodies are not as coordinated as they need them to be in order to make this happen.

Once he has got the sunglasses on, his intense look changes into smiles and his body is more relaxed.

Using the 12 features of play in the analysis

* The boy using the sunglasses as a play prop still needs plenty of first-hand experiences, out of which he will build his play so that he can move beyond the here and now. In this example, we have seen him initiate relating to people, playing with sunglasses. (Feature 1)

* He makes his own rules, which he applies over and over again. He keeps control of what he does and will not tolerate interference in this from anyone. At the moment he uses these rules as an unalterable sequence. He simply takes the sunglasses from his key person's nose and puts them on himself, then looks round. He then takes them off and puts them back on her. It is as if he is practising putting them off and on, and just acknowledging that he has seen people looking around when wearing them. He cannot transform his images and change them about. Play will open up the possibility to do this. (Feature 2)

* He uses anything that comes to hand as a play prop, but he doesn't make his own yet. Play props help him to remember images in his mind and give him prompts about what to do next as he begins to think forward. (Feature 3)

* He chooses whether to play or not. He is really in the mood to play at this time. He is like the babies and toddlers in previous chapters in that he would not be able or willing to play if he felt uncomfortable, hungry or tired. (Feature 4)

* Role play does not appear on this afternoon. He is rehearsing to be an adult wearing sunglasses, but he is not yet taking on the role of being someone else. (Feature 5)

* He is not pretending yet. This process develops as the child becomes a symbol user. He is already interested in the symbols of his culture. Symbols are a way of making one thing stand for another. At the moment, he is using the sunglasses to stand for doing what adults do. This kind of play will help him into more abstract thinking. Then he will be able to pretend all kinds of things in his play. (Feature 6)

* He will now play alone at times, but only if a trusted adult is near. (Feature 7)

* He loves to play with other children and with adults. When he is at home, he expects to lead his own play. This allows him to use to the full the images he has from his experiences. When adults impose their images on a child's play, the play cannot develop as easily; it is constrained. When adults encourage the child's images, by supporting and extending them, they deepen the play. (Feature 8)

* He is eager to play with an adult. She is very clear that she wants to play with him and respects the fact that his play agenda is beautifully strong. His play agenda fits well with his biological need to develop hand control and to be able to coordinate in order to put the sunglasses on. (Feature 9)

* He wallows in his play. He concentrates deeply in different play episodes. (Feature 10)
* He is trying out his latest learning as he plays. He shows both biological and socio-cultural competencies as he plays. (Feature 11)
* Through his play, he coordinates what he knows about grip, release, watching where moving objects go, balance, rotation, how adults behave when they see him with an object which is delicate and easily broken. This helps him to go beyond the here and now. (Feature 12)

He shows most of the 12 features in his play. He has yet to develop those which involve him in abstract thinking, that is, being a symbol user in a world of pretend and role play.

Children who are beginning to walk, communicate in words or signs and imitate what they see others do and wear are very much in a state of transition from toddler times. They love to hold or touch a different object with each hand.

In the photographs, the children have gathered together with their key people at the end of the morning for some songs. They are singing finger

Figure 5.7: The children have to concentrate hard to move their fingers into the correct positions. This coordination of looking, moving, listening and singing will help their later reading and writing.

Figure 5.8 – 5.9: The boy chooses to hold two wooden eggs. He is staying in his comfort zone, tired at the end of an active morning. But he is not passive. He joins in the larger actions, holding the eggs as he does so.

Figure 5.10: The adult leads the baby through the song and the baby is interested and looking intently. Finger rhymes have detail in them, and if introduced early, children can be helped to enjoy this aspect of singing, which helps them to look for small details with pleasure and intense focus.

rhymes, which are quite intricate to perform for young children, and take great concentration to learn and then sing and enact. But children are proud of their efforts and successes and the songs make an invaluable transition into building characters in small and manageable stories (Bruce and Spratt, 2011c). 'Two little birds sitting on a wall' is a finger rhyme showing how the fingers are not long fingers but transformed into birds that sit on the wall and fly away and come back, like homing pigeons.

A group of children are playing together. Gaia (seven years) and Hanja (five years) were spending the afternoon with Andy (seven years) and David (seven years). Gaia wanted to play hospitals, but the boys did not. She suggested that the boys go off to war and that she and Hanja would be nurses in the army hospital.

Key message
Biological and socio-cultural influences
Both the biological and the socio-cultural strands of development influence the possibility of children learning deeply through their play.

Each has an impact on the way that children are able to transform their images and imitate people and what they do, so that they are increasingly able to think in the past, present and future.

Summary

During the first three years, children develop a sense of their identity. They work out the concepts of 'I', 'me' and 'you'. This helps them to go beyond themselves in their ideas, feelings and relationships.

Beginning to talk in words or signs helps this process along.

Being able to think in images, to reconstruct the past and imagine the future, means they begin to move away from living mainly in the present.

They imitate things as they happen, but they also reconstruct what they saw people do on previous occasions, such as play football or read a book.

Gradually, their thinking happens less and less in separate images. Images become transformed and can be changed and altered during the thinking. Play helps this more flowing process of imaging to develop.

Children begin to develop play scenarios rehearsing adult roles, pretending, and finding and making play props. They become symbols users.

Play helps toddlers to move from the here and now, and so they can think in more abstract ways which increasingly involve the past and the future.

REFLECTIVE QUESTIONS FOR YOUR PRACTICE

Observe toddlers. Do they want to use the objects and clothes they see adults and older children using and wearing? Mobile phones? Hats? Bags? Money in a purse? Sunglasses?

In what way do toddlers show they are beginning to engage in symbolic, pretend play? Through imitation of what they see adults or older children doing? Do they take on a character yet? Or are they themselves being like someone and imitating their actions?

6 Observing, supporting and extending play (toddlers and young children)

Making friends with adults and children

In this chapter, we shall consider some of the ways in which children growing up in the UK are supported and helped to make friends and to deepen their play with others, both at home and in group settings.

Children vary in the ease with which they feel relaxed with people who are new to them. Some babies are very cuddly and enjoy being held and passed to different people. Others are more reserved. Our personalities are affected by these aspects of our temperaments throughout our lives.

We need to respect children's feelings as we help them to feel comfortable about widening the circle of adults and children that they play with.

Parents supporting play in the home

Adults are very important to young children. This is because, in the context of the UK, they help children to develop access strategies (Corsaro, 1979). Access strategies help children to join each other's play.

Some social situations which adults and children alike may find difficult include:

* joining a group
* being joined by other people.

For example, you might have been invited to a party. You know the hosts but none of their friends. You arrive on your own. What would help to make you feel comfortable?

Most people find it useful to be introduced to other guests by the host. This is because the host knows your interests and those of their other friends. Shared interests can be a useful bridge, helping you to find some common ground. For example, you and a fellow guest might both enjoy dancing or photography.

Some access strategies for adults to help children settle

Children who feel churned up inside find it difficult to become settled enough to play. The brain releases a chemical called cortisol when we are anxious, in order to put us on alert. But it means that we are not open and relaxed, which we need to be in order to learn. This contrasts with oxytocin, which when it is released in the brain opens us up to deep learning, and play is part of this.

Adults who know the child can help by:

* letting the child stay near physically
* getting down to the child's level
* encouraging the child to look at their face and keeping eye contact
* knowing the child's interests
* using what the child is interested in to help them settle
* staying physically near but keeping quiet as the child begins to reach out and talk with other people.

(Bruce *et al.*, 2010b)

These strategies are useful to parents, but they are just as useful to practitioners (especially the key person) in early years settings. The importance for young children of a close, continuous relationship with a small number of main carers, normally parents and close family members, cannot be overemphasised. The key person develops attachment (based on Bowlby's (1953) theory) between the child and particular members of staff (Elfer and Grenier, 2010).

Settling children in group settings

Relaxing enough to play

Joining a group is an emotional experience. The time it takes for children to feel part of things – to feel able to play – varies enormously. Other children help new children to settle, but adults are able to help children feel included in deep and important ways. Examples of things adults can do are:

* visiting the child and family before the child joins the group
* making sure a member of the family the child feels close to stays for the first fortnight or so and withdraws gradually
* having something, such as a particular toy, in the group setting which the child is known to like
* supporting the child with access strategies (outlined above) so that the child gains confidence and joins in.

Figures 6.1 – 6.2:   This little boy feels safe and secure in the nursery. He comes to the Jabadao Developmental Movement session without his key person, a session led by another member of staff. He is clearly enjoying the play. (Greenland (2010))

Figures 6.3 – 6.4: Some children are relaxed and opened up to learning enough to be fully involved in their collaborative and cooperative play. The boy with the practitioner is new to the group and understandably anxious, but he is being sensitively supported so that he can begin to relax and become involved at his own pace, in his own way.

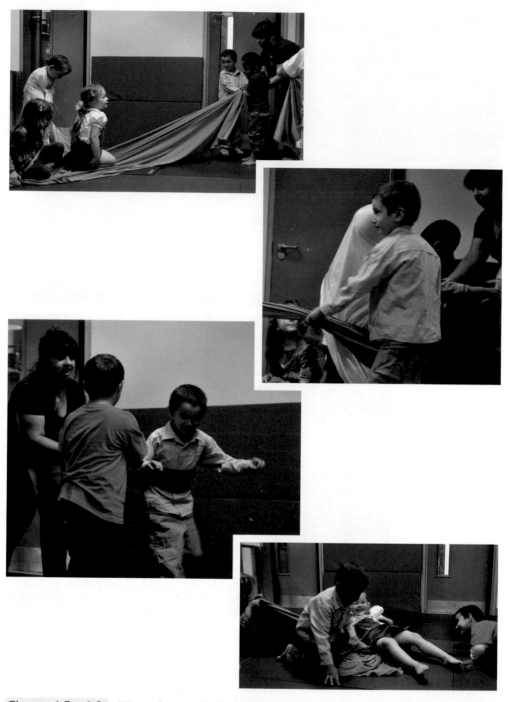

Figures 6.5 – 6.8: We see him gradually becoming part of the play. It is a great effort for him, and emotionally a huge experience, but it is clear that deep down he is pleased with himself and that his entry into group play is a positive experience, supported by the very skilled practitioner. She knows when to be with him and when to be near him with a watchful eye.

> ## Key message
> Once children feel included, play begins to develop.

An example of outdoor play

Play should be supported both indoors and outdoors.

Outdoor play

Children use nature in the garden in different ways. Sometimes they use leaves and twigs as props, but in the photographs in Figures 6.9–6.11 they are using the bushes and cushions as props. The bushes in the garden are anchor points they move in relation to, and the cushions are carried about to different points, behind, around, between bushes.

Play will always ebb and flow. There will be quiet, still times and noisy boisterous times. It is quite difficult to sustain free-flow play (Bruce, 1991, 2004, 2011b; Bruce et al., 2010b). So, regularly, children will peel off and take a few minutes quietly doing something different before rejoining the group. The children run about with friends, moving along in lines side by side, or following one another. Leaders emerge, who then become followers. There is awareness of others, but not much is said. There is a lot of quiet smiling and, from time to time, laughter. This opens children up to learning (Trevarthen, 1998).

Groups of children demonstrate in their play that they can coordinate their movements together. This will be invaluable to them if, in their later schooling, they play music in a group, dance in a group, or become involved in drama improvisations. It will also be useful in playing team sports, such as football, netball or hockey.

> ## Key message
> The ebb and flow of play enables children to develop their learning.
> Teaching is about observing, supporting and extending play and all kinds of learning (Bruce, 1987).

Figures 6.9 – 6.11: The children are engaged in follow-my-leader play, sometimes with the cushions on their heads, sometimes in front. The one behind imitates and follows. But at a certain point, he turns and changes direction, going round the bushes a different way. Then the one who was leading becomes the follower. Nothing is said, but they seem to be very aware, as they keep glancing at each other and are sensitive to changes in the movements and different ways in which their play partner holds their cushion.

How to support play (3–7 years of age)

Figure 6.12:   The girl has put pretend water in the saucepan and boiled it. She has added pasta and now she is stirring it to see if it is ready.

A group of children, all of whom had eaten pasta, decided to play at cooking. A three-year-old girl knew how to make it because she had eaten it at home and helped with the meal preparation. Most early pretend play arises out of everyday events, especially cooking and, nowadays, talking on the mobile phone. The girl initiated this food preparation play simply by re-enacting this everyday event realistically. She was quickly joined by other children. She needed to lead the play because she was the only one who had been involved in the cooking of pasta. Although she is engaging in pretend play, this is in the early stages still. She is imitating (being like) her mother cooking the pasta. She is not yet taking on a character, or developing a story – that will be the next stage in her pretend play.

A group of children, seven- to nine-year-olds, also played offices, but they made an advance plan together. They worked out who they would be (characters) and a story or narrative (plot). They dressed up and made play props for the different characters. They came to pay bills, sign cheques, write to people, telephone the bank. They were the office for a dress shop called 'Lady Jane'. There was a complaints department, an orders department and a sales department. These were all based on their real experiences of shopping, offices and the gas board showroom (hence the complaints department).

Figures 6.13 – 6.14: She decides it is ready and finds a colander. The other children want to help and she lets them. They chat about it. It is pretend water.

These examples show how children use their real-life experiences in their play. The imagination is the rearrangement of past experience in new ways, with new connections. The examples also show how biological age impacts on play. The one-year-old plays offices in a very different way from the seven-year-old, the four-year-old or the three-year-old.

When people say children learn entirely through play, they are saying something highly inaccurate. Play is central to learning, but it is not the only way children learn. Children also learn by watching other children, observing adults, imitating what they see, through their senses, by joining in games such as 'Snakes and Ladders', through first-hand experiences such as cooking, and through direct teaching.

Figures 6.15 – 6.16: She manages to serve it without spilling any.

Staff in early childhood group settings need to organise the day so that the natural ebb and flow of play episodes and scenarios can be supported. If children are not free to pace their play, the quality of play drops. Children need to intersperse their intense free-flow play with some of these other ways of learning, and with rest. But if children are always in situations where adults control what they do, they become constrained in their learning.

Childhood play will turn into adult creativity and imagination, but only if it is encouraged. It can be extinguished or diminished if it is not supported or extended. Imagination develops well if children are offered and engage with rich experiences involving the senses and movement, communication, and possibilities to represent these in many forms. The imagination (see Chapter 5) has been described by Peter McKellar (1957) as the rearrangement of past experience in new and fascinating ways. Creativity is mainly a process for young children, but there will be products sometimes, too (Bruce, 2011a).

Figures 6.17 – 6.18: The practitioner begins to eat with a pretend spoon. The little girl is not sure about this. She is at the stage where she needs realistic props, so she goes to find the practitioner a spoon.

Leo (four years) and Jason (six years) made a den in the garden. They knew how to put sticks together and tie them in a tepee style. They knew they needed two blankets to cover this and how to join the blankets with safety pins. Jason could sew tapes onto the opening and Leo wanted to tie those to shut the door. They spent ages in the preparation of their play props, but not so much time actually playing. The play itself was mostly about going out and shooting animals for supper and then pretending to eat them in the den. There were pretend night times with constant attacks from wild animals to wake them up.

When adults provide a varied play environment with opportunities to learn in all the different ways, they enable children to develop their learning. Helen Tovey (2007) emphasises the importance of outdoor play. The most important ways to support play are:

* to structure the environment so that it is conducive to the occurrence of play and play is more likely to arise
* for an adult to take an interest and be part of the play in a background way
* for the adult to be sensitive and aware of how to help things along without taking over.

Supporting an activity – playing shop

One of the most important things about extending play is not to over-structure it. If adults lead the play all the time, the child's imagination and creativity will shut down.

However, leaving children entirely without help to extend their play means the imagination and creativity that might have developed do not develop. This is because children don't know enough about how to free-flow play imaginatively.

Play doesn't always just happen – it needs people who help it along. This means developing the skill to support and extend play, informed by careful observation.

Through a shop-play scenario, following a visit to a real shop, adults can provide appropriately for children's play. The play environment can be carefully structured to encourage role play. Creating stories requires children to become characters and make up a storyline (narrative). But the children cannot write down their stories yet. Neither are they ready for adults to write down their stories, because they are only just learning what is involved in making a story. The shop-play scenario will help them towards this. It takes years of practice making play scenarios before the child writes down rich stories.

Indirect teaching is powerful

Our teaching grows out of our observations of individual children whom we know well and because of this we can enable them to learn. Teaching responds to this – sometimes in very direct ways, sometimes indirectly.

For example, we may be watching a child who is struggling to use scissors. Perhaps their current inability to master cutting is holding back their play. They can't make the prop for their dragon's head dress. We may show the child that it is easier to use scissors if we hold them in a certain way. This is direct teaching.

We may have observed another child who is already very good at using scissors. Perhaps we have noticed that they have a particular interest in cutting different materials. We might decide to structure a play environment that would enable the child to explore their interest in depth. Perhaps a workshop or post office area would give them some exciting opportunities. This is indirect teaching.

Indirect teaching strategies are especially powerful because they allow flexibility and encourage children to use initiative and be active learners. Indirect teaching strategies often lead to children gaining knowledge and understanding that the adult had not intended to teach. This is very exciting and makes teaching both fun and deeply satisfying. What could be better than to find that children have learned more than you directly taught them?

An example could be that a child who finds it difficult to sit quietly and listen to a story enters into the role play. They are the customer 'in a rush to do the shopping'. By becoming involved in a way in which they are capable, the child becomes engaged and concentrates deeply.

A child is much more likely to enjoy story time with the group after plenty of experience making up stories through play scenarios. In fact, the child is likely to use some of the ideas from stories they listen to in their play scenarios.

Indirect teaching has a powerful effect on learning.

Practical ways to extend play

Key message

There are two important aspects to extending free-flow play and so developing well-planned play:

1. Extending the material provision.
2. Conversations with children about the things that adults do, such as cooking and shopping.

Extending the material provision

Having made a basic shop for the children to play with, adults can extend the provision based on what they have observed has already piqued the children's interest. For example, perhaps:

* the bags and baskets are well used
* so are the objects for sale
* the children pretend to use money.

Leading on from these observations, we could make some or all of the following changes to our provision:

* There could be a variety of bags. Paper bags of different sizes could be offered and carrier bags provided (carefully supervised and never left unattended). Bags would be beautifully presented, perhaps hanging on a hook on the wall, or in neat boxes on the counter. Children could choose a bag to put their shopping in.

* There could be a weighing machine and a balance. Although children do not yet understand the calibrations on such equipment, they benefit from learning that it helps us to know how heavy something is. They might pick out numbers. They will understand more easily later on that the arm of the balance will be straight if two things are the same weight.

  Although they do not understand the concept of weight yet, they do have a sense of balance and symmetry. This will help them to develop a concept of weight in the long term. Play is an important vehicle for reflecting on such things without pressure to perform.

  It looks as if children are just messing about with balances and weighing machines, but they are experimenting and exploring, musing about things in ways which will build into higher concepts, such as weight and number.

* A cash machine could be made out of a box. Coins could be made out of cardboard. When adults make play props, they are being good role models for creativity. Children can be encouraged to add their props, too. For example, one child might pick up a piece of card and 'swipe' it over the counter. They have created a credit card.

* Children might enjoy being shop assistants who have to put prices or bar codes on the articles for sale. Having some sticky labels could be very exciting.

* Having a price list – with a picture of each object for sale and a price next to it – encourages children to play with numbers. This could be in the form of a book, or on a piece of stiff cardboard.

* There could be a window display in the shop. A child who wants to be part of the play but who needs to be alone in the play scenario might find this a good way to join in. They would need drapes and perhaps torches to spotlight the objects on display.

* The objects for sale could be extended. Many children play at supermarkets as this tunes into their experiences. Empty packets of cereal, stuffed with newspaper to keep the shape, and pretend tins of food in the shape of cylinders are popular. These can be made from offcuts of wood. Some children might enjoy drawing pictures on them (felt pens are good for this) to show the food that is in the pretend tin. Older children might enjoy making labels from rectangles of paper, drawing pictures of the food and then sticking them on the cylinder. But this requires considerable skill and is not easy for young children (3–6 years). It would be an enjoyable extension for older children (7–11 years).

＊ Foods such as cheese can be made using dough. Children enjoy using wire-cutters to cut the pretend cheese and placing it on greaseproof paper or polythene sheets to be weighed.

They can also make fruit and vegetables, fish and meat out of the dough. There might be a table or workshop area near to the shop where children could do this. They could even play out a scenario at a bread factory. Buns, rolls, bread, biscuits and cakes could be set out on trays to be taken from the factory to the shop.

＊ Some children might enjoy transporting the goods from the factory and delivering them to the shop using a cart and pretending to drive it.

＊ Some children might enjoy dressing up as the different characters who visit the shop. So, having a dressing-up corner near the shop would be helpful. Adults might need to role model this and pretend to be a customer coming to the shop. Children might appreciate realistic paper hats to wear when serving at the cheese counter.

There are times when children are ill and need to stay quiet. Mannie (seven years) was in bed for several weeks, unable to move about very much. Her mother brought her a box of dolls from several countries which she had collected when she was a child. They decided where these dolls would live on the bed. For example, the Swiss doll was put on top of Mannie's legs (on a mountain) and the Dutch doll was put at her feet to represent a flat countryside.

Continuous provision

There should always be a core of open-ended provision that is offered continuously. This means that is constantly available. Other experiences can be added in or changed, and may not be offered all day and every day.

Examples of continuous provision are:

＊ malleable natural materials (clay, mud, dough)
＊ workshop area, with found and recycled materials for model making, construction and mark making
＊ home corner for domestic play
＊ small world play (dolls' house, garage, farm, prehistoric animals, roads, trains)
＊ sand (wet and dry) and water
＊ wooden blocks (mini, unit and hollow)
＊ dens indoors and outdoors
＊ book corner with fiction and non-fiction
＊ cookery area
＊ woodwork area.

The outdoor area is as important as the indoor area and makes up half the learning space.

Extending play by sensitively joining the child or children

Some very important issues are emerging from our consideration of the play provision.

* Children will not extend into rich, free-flow play unless they are helped to do so, because it is too difficult.
* Play leads them into abstract thinking, which is not easy to do. Therefore, adults need to join the play.
* They need to join the play in ways which do not take it over, but which help the children to become as independent in their play as possible.
* Children who extend their play have their own ideas, play out their own feelings and explore the relationships they have with others. They are not dependent on adults for their thinking. They become autonomous learners, who can get on with learning without waiting for adults to tell them what to do, think, feel, or how to relate to others. They are in control, and able to learn in deep ways in their play.
* Children are helped to extend their play if they have play props, but the play props need to be open ended. Commercially made props have limited value and are expensive. They encourage only a narrow response from children. A plastic apple is usually played with as if it is an apple; a child can make whatever fruit or vegetable they want with a lump of dough!
* Props made by the children to serve their imaginative and creative ideas, feelings and relationships with others are richer than any other kind of prop for extending play.
* Some children do not have to rely on props very much at all. They can pretend, and often use mime and movement, for example to pretend pouring tea into an imaginary cup.

How adults can extend the play by sensitively joining in

Adults playing with young children will use one of three strategies. Sometimes they are conscious of these, sometimes not. Adults who are informed about the way children develop find it easier to extend play than those who are not.

Most adults rely on remembering their own childhood play and passing on what they learned about it as children to the next generation. There will be a huge cultural dimension in this. Some adults will have learned about play from adults; others will have learned about it from other children.

Strategy one – interest and imitation

This can take two forms:

1. Some adults might simply be there and look interested. Children are then highly likely to draw them into the play.
2. They might imitate what the experienced player does.

Strategy two – by invitation

Another strategy for extending play is to just be there, but not taking an obvious interest unless invited. This is important if the child moves into free-flow play, needing privacy and no interruptions. These moments of flow are deep for the child and may be quite fleeting or of sustained length. This is where adults need to be very sensitive and able to tune into the child's play needs.

Strategy three – conversation

A third and important strategy for extending play is through conversations with children. For example, in shop play, the adult pretends to buy provisions. An important aspect of play is that it should be clear to everyone playing what the play scenario is about. This means that everyone who wants to join in can. The play scenario's theme usually begins with an 'announcement'. For example, a child might say, 'Let's play shops.' This gives a play theme that children can join in with, or not, as they wish. There is no reason why an adult should not make an 'announcement' and offer a play scenario scene. The adult might say something like, 'I'm going to play shopping.'

Once the play scenario has a theme which everyone knows about, the adult can say something like, 'I am going to be the mum, so I'm going to put on my hat because it's cold outside.' Children are likely to join in. Hopefully, they will begin to voice their play agenda and develop their ideas. As this begins to happen, the adult can hold back more and more, staying in the background unless needed. The more the adult is needed in the play scenario, the lower the level of play will be.

The play might look quite exciting to an outsider, but this is because the adult will be making up a good storyline about shopping. The adult will be helping children to move into their roles, pretending to be shopkeepers, or customers, or factory workers, or delivery people. The adult might be helping children to stay in role, so that they stay in the character for a sustained time. But if it all depends on the adult, then it only shows that the adult can engage children in rich free-flow play; it does not mean that the children can manage it on their own.

The adult should aim not to withdraw from the play, because staying in the play shows that adults value it, but to take an increasingly backstage part.

Adults as catalysts for free-flow play

Adults need to become play catalysts, rather than keeping children dependent on them in their play. If free-flow play is encouraged, then children are likely to turn into good creative story writers in middle childhood. This is because they will know:

* how to create a character
* how to develop the character's adventures
* how to create an interesting story and take it to the end
* how to make the different characters interact.

> **Key message**
> **The 12 features of play**
>
>   1. Using first-hand experiences.
>   2. Making up rules.
>   3. Making props.
>   4. Choosing to play.
>   5. Rehearsing the future.
>   6. Pretending.
>   7. Playing alone.
>   8. Playing together.
>   9. Having a personal agenda.
> 10. Being deeply involved.
> 11. Trying out recent learning.
> 12. Coordinating ideas, feelings and relationships for free-flow play.
>
> (Adapted from Bruce 1991, 2010a)

Getting into role is a real challenge. This is why play props and dressing-up clothes are so helpful. Looking like or feeling like the character helps. Pretending to be everyday people is easier than trying to be a spaceman, superhero or heroine (Holland, 2003). This is because children can use their real-life experience to base the character on, e.g. Daddy washing up.

Once the child is dressed up and ready to play but perhaps doesn't know how to start play flowing, the adult can help by getting the two characters to talk to each other. The adult, who is pretending to be the mum, might say something like, 'I've got to buy some potatoes today. My children keep wanting chips for supper. Do your children ask you for their favourite meals?' The child can then reply in the role of neighbour, but with plenty of opportunities to develop their own ideas.

Play, creativity and imagination

Imagination

The links between play, creativity and imagination are strong. Imagination arises out of the images that children form. And images of all kinds (tactile, olfactory, taste, sight and sound) are ways in which the brain can keep hold of real experiences. At first, images are separate, not joined together, but once images become mobile, children can experience flights of imagination.

Imagination is important because it is the way that the human brain puts together and rearranges experiences in new ways. The imagination transforms experience and supports creativity.

In their pretend play, we see children beginning to develop imagination. One minute they are eating a real apple, the next they are eating a pretend one. Play supports the development of the imagination in ways which are right for children.

Creativity

Creativity takes the ordinariness out of life and makes it more satisfying. The psychologist Winnicott (1974) suggests that creativity belongs to the feeling of 'being alive'.

In order to be creative, children need to feel emotionally safe enough to make new connections, new directions and new insights. This is where play is a powerful support to creativity. Play gives children the positive personal space to be alone with themselves, while at the same time feeling connected to other people, especially those who are important to them emotionally. In their play, children dare to be different and to try out alternative worlds, to explore – what if this happened, etc.

Play helps children with creative processes. Children gather ideas, sort out and manage feelings, learn about the physical body they inhabit and then incubate them. Ideas hatch in play, but without the constraints of making an end product (a creation). Every child, including those with special educational needs, learning difficulties and disabilities, can be creative. Play helps this along in deep and important ways.

Steven (seven years) and Ann (six years) played butterflies one summer afternoon. They followed each other about, pretending to land on flowers and dancing. They had scarves as wings, which they held with their hands, and flapped their arms up and down.

Summary

In this chapter, we have looked at how adults can both support play and extend it into the highest levels of free-flow play. When adults observe, support and extend children's learning through well-planned play, they are teaching.

Children at play coordinate their ideas, feelings and make sense of relationships with their family, friends and culture. When play is coordinated it flows along in a sustained way. It is called free-flow play (Bruce, 1991).

We have looked at how to observe, support and extend play. We have seen how children draw on real-life experience and use this in their play themes and the characters they begin to create.

We have seen how we can help and support play to extend into a world of imagination and pretend by providing an enabling environment. This should not be a miniature real world, but an environment in which props are suggestions and prompts for children's feelings, ideas and relationships and physical, moving selves. Then children can transform their thoughts through deep and empowering play. They can begin to make sense of their experiences, to apply what they know and understand, and reflect on how things are, how they could be and how they can be managed.

REFLECTIVE QUESTIONS FOR YOUR PRACTICE

Audit the continuous material indoors and outdoors. This might be in a group setting, or in a home learning environment. How much are the children given opportunities to experience and play with these without being directed to use the materials in adult-controlled and specified ways?

Useful texts to help you in considering the experiences offered to children daily include:

Bruce, T. Meggitt, C. And Grenier, J. (2010b) *Child Care and Education*, 5th edn, Hodder Education: London.

Core Experiences for the Early Years Foundation Stage, September 2009, available from Early Education, www.early-education.org.uk.

Does the material provided and the way children are encouraged to use it support play, imagination and creativity?

To read more about creativity, see:

Bruce, T. (2011a) *Cultivating Creativity in Babies, Toddlers and Young Children*, Hodder Education: London.

7 How play helps children to understand other people

Childhood play enables children to be at their best.

Learning about good and bad

As they deepen their play, children become philosophers, struggling with what is good and what is evil. They reflect on what makes people kind, and what it means to treat people with fairness. Are you a baddie if you didn't mean to hurt someone? Do you become a baddie if you meant to do harm? How do other people react to kindness? What should people do if others cheat them, hit them, trick them, or help them? All of these philosophical themes, exploring morality and justice, can be found in childhood play.

The themes which children develop in their play scenarios contribute to their personal, social and emotional development.

Of course, we go on trying to work out what is right or wrong for all of our lives. Right and wrong can be one of the most difficult distinctions to make.

Learning about feelings

Feelings run deep in play. The great themes of literature across the world are played out: there are sad and joyful meetings and partings, terrifying and daring raids; there are situations which involve creeping up on people and surprising them, operating in gangs, being abandoned, being caught, being rescued and being helped and protected. All of this is very emotional, but it also contributes to an understanding of story and narrative.

Coping with life

In their play, children face the difficulties of their lives. They deal with their feelings. They find ways of coping with situations or people that hurt their feelings, or make them angry. They come to terms with their lives, or find ways of changing them as they experiment in their play with different ways of relating to people.

Childhood play helps children to learn that different people have different ideas. It helps them to get inside other people's heads, feelings and relationships.

Observing sympathy overcome anxiety

Every child who attends a group setting has experienced being new in the group. They know how it feels to be with people you don't yet know well and to wonder how they will treat you. They may have had positive experiences, where they have been gently introduced to the way the group works, in an atmosphere of warmth and affection. They may have been helped to make friends. In this case, they might enjoy helping a new child by doing the same for them.

Alternatively, they may have felt anxious, having to find their own way into the group, copying what the other children do in order to learn how things are done and in the hope of making some friends. It might have been hard not to feel unsettled, sad and lonely, and even frightened at times.

However, there is something else which play helps children to develop, something that develops out of sympathy. This means understanding how someone else feels. It means that children begin to be able to recognise that you might think or feel differently about something from me, as we saw briefly in the Introduction. This is called 'theory of mind'. But it begins with a child understanding how they themselves might feel in a particular situation (which is the ability to decentrate). We might say to a toddler, 'Would you like it if Jo squeezed your arm?'

In the photograph, the toddler is walking with pleasure along the hollow blocks with the key person. This 'road' was built by another, older child, who gave permission for this little one to walk along the top once it was made. This was only while they went to find some cars to put out on the road. Children learn to be kind as they play.

Figure 7.1: Walking on the road.

Playing in pairs

When children play, they need to be fine-tuned to each other's thinking and feelings. If they aren't, then the play will fade. Children don't want that to happen, they are enjoying it so much. They want to keep the play free flowing along. Their pleasure in this play is not simply jolly fun, it is deeper than that. As they play together, perhaps with the toy cars, they have adventures with ideas which are stimulating and exciting.

* They confirm their belief that cars go down slopes. One day they will use the word gravity.
* They see that a slope breaks a fall, so that the cars do not crash to the ground but move along gently from a height to the roof of the trailer.
* They see how the groove on the ramp stops the cars from falling off as they travel downwards. These grooves are different from the train rails that keep trains on a track. The car wheels slot into the grooves on the trailer. The wheels on the train have grooves that slot over the train tracks. These sorts of things fascinate children. They may seem to be tiny details, but they embody important scientific concepts for young children to explore.
* As they play together, they are working out how the other is thinking and feeling. They are trying to understand each other. They find that, if they take turns, it goes well.
* They find that they both have a similar play agenda. Probably, each boy would like to have all the turns, but they have both worked out that, if they did that, it wouldn't be much fun for the other person, who might leave the play.
* They are willing to give up doing exactly as they want and to think about what the other person wants, because the other person has good ideas that make the play go deeper.
* If they use each other's ideas, they develop a better play scenario.
* In order to develop rich, cooperative play, children need to be aware of how other children are thinking and feeling. They need to recognise that someone may have similar ideas but that someone else might have very different ideas.

Maria (five years) is playing in the home area. She answers the telephone and pretends to talk to her friend. 'Yes. Come over for a cup of tea. That will be nice. See you soon.' She puts the phone down. The friend arrives and knocks on the door. Maria answers and lets her friend in. She can't find any cups and saucers in the dresser. She goes to the phone and picks it up. 'Hello. Is that the shop? I need some more cups. Do you have some? Yes. Thank you. I will come to your shop now.' She goes out of the house, leaving her friend. Her friend sits at the table for a while but then goes to the dough table where she begins to become involved in making pretend cakes. She does not return to the home area.

If Maria had found cups in the home area, the play might not have faded in the way that it did. Boundaries need to be set about the removal of crockery from the home area. A picnic set with old pieces can be provided to take out of the area.

Children's roles in play

Children who lead the play

Children who are leaders in play are well developed in their understanding and awareness of others. In fact, if we observe closely, we find that one of the two boys playing with toy cars is leading the play scenario. He later leads the play outside in the garden, and seems to take care of the boy who is new. In both situations he is careful not to dominate the play. He makes all the suggestions about what to do, but he makes sure that his friend has plenty of turns with the cars, and feels as if he is actively participating.

There is a difference between dominating and leading the play.

Decentration

This is about the ability to put **yourself** into someone else's head and to imagine how you would feel and think. But this is based on the idea, 'How would I feel in this situation?' It is different from 'theory of mind' because that means being able to imagine how someone else (not you) might feel in a situation, and the realisation that not everyone feels or thinks in the same way. Children who lead the play (Rubin, 1983) are good at decentring.

Theory of mind

This is recognising that someone feels and thinks differently from the way you do. A child who has theory of mind can work out how to develop the play with a partner, or even with a whole group.

Free-flow play is an invaluable preparation for adult life because it enables children to develop theory of mind.

Sympathy

This is recognising how someone else feels because you have similar feelings. It means you know how you would like to be treated. This links with the expression that you should always try to 'do as you would be done by'.

Figure 7.2: The boys move together, in tune with each other, which is necessary for play to flow. They are thinking about and are aware of each other as they play.

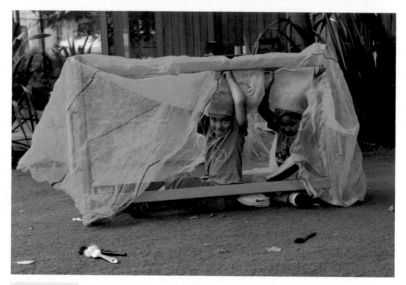

Figure 7.3: They lift the roof together and have to concentrate.

There are times when children want to be joined in their play, but the painting-the-house idea worked best when it was just the two boys (see Figures 7.4–7.7). This is one of the things that practitioners need to bear in mind when children spend whole days in group provision. Children need to be able to make choices and to develop their play themes without frustration. Sometimes their play needs to be protected by adults and sometimes they use strategies to protect it themselves. It would not be right always to insist that children share.

Figures 7.4 – 7.5: The boy who is nearest the brushes reaches out for them and gives one to his friend. They pretend to paint their house.

It is important to note that the adults were always near when this free-flow play got under way, but did not disturb it during the five minutes it lasted. It suddenly faded and vanished, as free-flow play does. All the same, it is those magical few moments that we take with us through our lives and which prepare us well for adulthood.

Figures 7.6 – 7.7: They are joined by other children and the play fades. It simply no longer works. The other children leave quite soon, and the boys quickly sit in their house with their legs outstretched, so that there is no space for anyone to join them. They put down the flap to make a wall. A group of girls look, but they don't try to enter.

Using the 12 features of play in the analysis

* The boys have seen adults painting and decorating (for example, the caretaker in the school). (Feature 1)
* They make up some rules for being in their den, about when flaps are down and up, and whether they want to be joined in this small space. (Feature 2)
* They are using play props – the dens and the brushes. (Feature 3)
* They have chosen to play together and when and how to play. (Feature 4)
* They are rehearsing adult roles (painting and decorating) for the future. (Feature 5)
* They are pretending to be decorators of their house. (Feature 6)
* They are playing in a pair. (Feature 8)
* They have a shared play agenda and are enjoying doing the same things. (Feature 9)

> **Key message**
> **The 12 features of play**
>
>   1. Using first-hand experiences.
>   2. Making up rules.
>   3. Making props.
>   4. Choosing to play.
>   5. Rehearsing the future.
>   6. Pretending.
>   7. Playing alone.
>   8. Playing together.
>   9. Having a personal agenda.
>   10. Being deeply involved.
>   11. Trying out recent learning.
>   12. Coordinating ideas, feelings and relationships for free-flow play.
>
> (Adapted from Bruce 1991, 2010a)

* They have been frustrated in developing their play and so are not as deeply immersed in it as they might have been. (Feature 10)
* Because of this they are not showing their full knowledge of decorating and painting as they might have done. (Feature 11)

Once children move into territory guarding in their play, they do not deepen the quality of their play and do not bring the learning together.

Newcomers to play

Children who dominate the play

Domination is very different from being a leader of the play scenario. Children who dominate in group-play scenarios need adult help.

Maisie was four years old. She avoided any situation where she could not keep control. She was too anxious to be in situations where she felt a loss of control. This meant that she avoided contact with adults in the early years setting she attended, in case they took away her feeling of control and made her join their activities. She gathered children around her whom she could boss about, and changed the rules if any child began to threaten her feeling of total control. This was not a healthy situation.

This is the sort of situation which might lead to a child becoming a dictatorial leader of a gang.

> ### Key message
>
> If we want to produce children who are caring towards others, able to lead and contribute to their own and other communities in a fast-changing world, we need to encourage free-flow play. It helps children to have sympathy (empathy) for others and to respect the different ways that people think and feel.

How adults can help children who dominate the play

How could Maisie be helped? She needed an adult to join her play, do her bidding, without making her feel threatened. Once she became relaxed and confident in the relationship, the adult could help her to involve other children in her play in ways which would encourage her to understand how they feel.

For example, she might want to pretend to play at being a demanding customer in the shop. The adult could encourage her to include other children as customers, each with a different character. One might be fussy about how something is wrapped; one might be in a hurry; one might have children. The adult might make it fun for Maisie to try to jump the queue in the shop and see how the other characters react.

She would still be central in the story, but the adult would be helping her to see the advantages of letting other children contribute their play ideas. It would mean that the play scenario could develop a better story than it would have done. Over time, once Maisie begins to realise this, she will begin to include the play agendas of other children. Instead of using other children to fulfil her play ideas, she will move into cooperative play. Cooperative play means she will help each child in the play to bring their ideas and feelings. They will then develop the storyline together.

The adult participation in Maisie's play creates an appropriate stepping stone towards an early learning goal.

Notice that the way Maisie is supported in her play is quite different from that of other children. Every child is unique.

Helping yourself

Children do not always need an adult to help them sort out their challenges as they develop. In this chapter so far, we have seen with the example of den building that the boys managed to protect their play, and hopefully were able to reconnect with it after being disturbed.

Two girls are enjoying playing together in the sandpit. Another girl is watching from a little distance and would like to join in. She uses a classic access strategy. She sees that they have sand scoops, so she fetches one for herself and then joins them and does as they do. They welcome her into their play, as is usually the case when children join in with such skill.

Summary

Play helps children to:

* become more aware of others
* become more sensitive towards others
* imagine how you would feel in a situation (decentration)
* understand how others feel (sympathy)
* realise that other people have good ideas (theory of mind)
* recognise that their ideas might be similar from yours (theory of mind)
* understand that their ideas might be different from yours (theory of mind)
* find ways of using other people's ideas to make the play flow better (leadership and management).

In short, play helps children to understand themselves and other people.

REFLECTIVE QUESTIONS FOR YOUR PRACTICE

Observe children at play in a play scenario which involves pretend. How old are the children? Is this significant? Explain your thoughts.

Identify themes, such as good and evil.

What does the official document for your country say about play? Make links between your observations, this chapter which is based on research and theory, and the official document. Is there agreement?

8 Play is the highest form of learning in early childhood

It is in their play that children show their intelligence at the highest level of which they are capable. Play opens up new possibilities in thinking and develops the emotional intelligence that makes feelings manageable. It helps a sense of self and relationships with others to deepen. Froebel (1782–1852) pioneered the importance of play in early childhood education, and this was echoed later by Vygotsky (1896–1934).

Key message

Play enlarges the child's life, so that the child makes more of it.

Play takes children out of themselves

Play helps children to explore the world beyond themselves and what they know.

* It brings spiritual awareness by helping children to understand themselves, others and matters of the universe.
* It encourages imagination and creativity.
* It helps children to become symbol users.
* It helps children to develop deeper and deeper layers in their use of symbols, both of their own and of others.
* It develops abstract thinking, which goes beyond the here and now into the past, future and alternative worlds.

Play takes children out of themselves, so that they can think of others in ways which are deeply caring. Froebel believed that play lifted children to their highest levels of spiritual awareness. In modern terms, this means that play helps children to know themselves and others, and to relate to the universe they inhabit.

Play and creativity

Isadora Duncan (1930) was a creative dancer who devised new techniques that changed the face of Western dance for ever. She commented:

I wonder how many adults realise that by the so-called education they are giving their children, they are only driving them into the commonplace, and depriving them of any chance of doing anything beautiful or original.

The world, if it is to survive, needs people who have vision, who have the imagination to see how things could be developed, improved, made better – and the creativity to make his happen. Free-flow play helps children to develop this state of mind, because it helps them to develop a feeling of control over the frightening and stressful aspects of life, as well as giving them opportunities to experiment with different ways of living and different strategies for doing things.

Emily (six years) suggests they play rainforests. She has seen a television programme about Indians living in the rainforests of Brazil. She suggests they make a village. They all make a den together in the garden, scooping up grass cuttings from the recently mown lawn. They put these in a heap to mark a wall for a den. Jason (four years) becomes absorbed in doing this, but he keeps putting his scoops of grass in a bucket he finds. He tips the bucket into the den.

'No!' shouts Tracey (four years). 'You are spoiling our village!'

'I know,' says Emily, 'that can be the food we cook on our fire.'

Jason throws the next bucket load in another part of the den. 'Oh! He's spoiling our village,' cries Tracey. 'Stop it, Jason!'

Emily says, 'Jason, only put it here. Look, Jason, put it here. You can be the man who brings the food, but you must only put it here. Look, when you bring the food I am the Chief. I say, "Put it here" and you have to do it, because I am the Chief, and you have to do what I say.'

Jason laughs. He waits for her to say 'Put it here' and then runs away to scoop up more grass.

Tracey is the child who stays in the village. Sharon (five years) goes off and collects food, like Jason. She finds a teddy and brings it back, but she does not take it inside the den. She says, 'This is the goat. I am milking the goat. The goat has got to stay outside, doesn't he?' Emily says, 'Yes, and the Chief comes and says bring me some milk.' The play flows along. Emily has become the leader and eases the play through tricky moments to the satisfaction of all the players.

Free-flow play encourages us to get out of ourselves, onto a higher plane. It is difficult to describe what it feels like to be creative. Creating a dance in childhood play is a feeling as much as it is an idea. Most of the dance-like play young children engage in vanishes and fades as the play episode finishes, never to be repeated exactly. But it leaves behind traces that linger in the mind. Later in life, these might be taken up and adult dances might be choreographed. Music might be composed. Dramatic plays might be written. Jazz might be improvised. Poetry might be written. A scientific invention or theory might be made.

This is how, in the film, 12-year-old Billy Elliot describes what it feels like to make up a dance:

It sort of feels good . . . once I get going I forget everything . . . I start to disappear. I can feel a change in my whole body, like there's a fire in my body . . . Just there . . . A fire . . . like a bird . . . electricity . . . Yes, like electricity.

Human beings are not the only animals to develop symbolic behaviour. For example, chimpanzees do (Matthews, 2010). But humans develop symbolic behaviour in greater depth and range. It is, therefore, desirable not to constrain children in the development towards deeper and deeper layerings of symbolic behaviour

Humans have the possibility of becoming competent, versatile, imaginative and creative symbol users. This means that the anxieties and dangers that are inherent parts of being creative, but which are part of improving the world, can be eased through the laughter and cathartic experiences that become possible as childhood play gradually turns into adult creativity.

Widening the world

Adults working with other people's children will open up the thinking of the children they spend time with, if they embrace diversity in play and value it beyond the Western European cultural heritage and tradition (Bruce *et al.*, 2010b). Part of becoming a broad-minded and deep thinker involves appreciation of the symbolic behaviour of other cultures. In this way, children learn to see that to privilege the dominant Western European culture of the UK makes their lives narrower and culturally impoverished. Children growing up in a transglobal world will need diverse ways to become flexible, adaptive and creative symbol users. Play can make a huge contribution to this broadening process.

Learning to write

Enriching the experience through play

When children play at writing, they treat it as a problem-solving adventure. This is the approach that we will use here, as well as the way of most countries in the world. Encouraging play with writing may seem to take longer and even to waste time, but taking a long-term view leads to steady and lasting progress.

Children are offered plenty of opportunities to try things out, to explore, experiment, manipulate and discover the potential possibilities of pencils, scissors, glue and paper. Children are not rushed through their childhood; this is not a fast-track approach. There is as much emphasis on what is being written as on how it is written or how good the writing looks. It takes much longer to learn to write this way but, in the long run, it is more likely to turn children into enthusiastic writers and bookworms (Goouch and Lambirth, 2007).

Writing is part of a wider kind of learning

Malaguzzi (1996), the Italian educator, wrote about the 'hundred languages of the child'. Learning to write is just one part of becoming a symbol user, when children are encouraged to learn writing through play. Children learn to see writing as an important way of making one thing (the symbol) stand for another. But, because of their play, they realise that writing is not the only way.

Figure 8.1: Writing is not the only way in which children represent their experiences.

Drawing, dance, music and mathematical symbols (such as numbers and geometric shapes) are just as important as writing. This approach to learning to write (and read) values the arts and the sciences because they enrich how people write and read.

The mechanics of learning to write and read should not dominate the learning; this destroys deep learning. The story that is being written, or the story that is being read, matters more than how to form a letter or the correct spelling, at least when young children are first beginning to take the stories they have played or have listened to and put them down on paper.

Learning to write is difficult. Having time to play with every element involved in writing makes it deeply satisfying, so that the motivation to write lasts across the years and throughout life.

Vygotsky (1978) says that the drawings children do are the beginnings of their writing. Gradually, they put letter-like shapes into the drawing, which they then begin to move to the edge. They put these emergent letter shapes into rows, perhaps across the top of the page. Some of the letters look like real letters; some do not. Or, they might draw rows of zig-zag lines to represent writing.

Malaguzzi (1996) suggests that in their drawings and emergent writings children are exploring different ways of becoming a symbol user. Drawing (which will turn into writing) is one way. Learning to use the scissors is a

Figures 8.2 – 8.3: Sharing a book means that at times the story almost becomes play. Making the rocket take off is an action that is enjoyed together and brings alive the text of the book.

Figure 8.4: Climbing up to join the group for a story – with eagerness because the children know that stories are worth the effort. Stories that are read to children often become themes in their play scenarios.

different way of working with paper. These are two kinds of symbolic tool: the pencil and the scissors.

It is not easy to use a pencil or scissors when you are three years old. Children need a supportive adult to be near, encouraging them to play with the paper.

Children often enjoy cutting up their drawing. After all, they have created it, so if they choose to destroy it, that is fine. But are they destroying it? Every time they a piece off, the child is likely to hold it against the paper to make it whole again. It is a bit like a jigsaw. It is as if they are playing with the idea of the whole and the parts. Children understand this concept by the time they are seven or eight years old, but they begin to explore it long before then.

When children are drawing or cutting, they are rarely still or in one place – they are on the move, selecting pieces of paper to cut. It may look as if they are aimless, but play does not have a definite purpose. It takes children where they didn't know they were going. It takes them where they didn't know they could go. It takes them out of themselves and onto a higher plane.

From time to time, in order to play at the highest level, children need the support of their parent or key person – someone who cares about them and for whom they care. The adult might hold the paper taut, so that the child can use their latest and best cutting skills. The adult will move carefully, so as to give the child maximum help without undermining them. When this happens, the child feels very good about it and is pleased with their cutting.

Young children are not usually interested in producing a finished result. This is because play is a process, it is not concerned with products. It cannot be pinned down into an end result. That is why it is called free-flow play.

Play is not the same as recreation. Recreation is what you do after a hard day's play! Recreation is when children relax and switch off from the deep thinking they have been involved in during their play. Recreation is about having fun, whereas play is often about serious thinking, which may be deeply enjoyable and fun, but which could be quite painful. Play therapy can help children to deal with sadness and pain. However, as Anna Freud (in Bruce et al., 2010b) knew, for most children the day-to-day play that they engage in quite naturally enables them to cope with life and get things under control. Play has the power to self-heal hurt and pain.

Making a narrative

In Chapter 2 we looked at the work of Lilli Nielsen, who believes that children benefit from playing in the dens that they make. When children cannot make their own dens because they have a complex need and disability which constrains them physically, she builds their own 'Little Room' around them, so that they can have this experience. She observes the child carefully and makes a house which is based on things that interest the child. She hopes this will be a place the child enjoys and one which, through play, opens up their learning.

Children love to make their own play dens, and do so often. They sometimes make dens with friends, sometimes with parents, and sometimes alone.

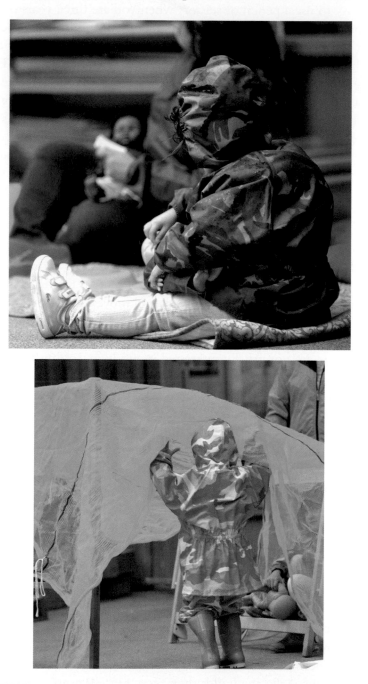

Figures 8.5 – 8.6:   At different points in the day, different children inhabit the den. Here two girls are playing in the den with the dolls. They have been playing with the dolls outside, and the practitioner has been helping them to dress the dolls and select clothes for them.

Figure 8.7: Boys and girls play together in the den.

Figure 8.8: The practitioner shows the boy how to tie the string to the den to stop it flapping.

Figure 8.9: The boy begins to work at tying the string to secure the den. He concentrates deeply.

Making a den – the first step to a story

Sometimes children choose to make a den out of a cardboard box. Abigail is very imaginative in her play. A cardboard box seems to provide her with a way of creating a story in her play scenario. She needs the box as a prop to get her started.

At first, she goes in and out of the box and experiments with it, supported in this by her mother. The mood is one of play, but she isn't yet free flowing. She's limbering up, ready to flow!

It is very important, at this point, for an adult to let her take the lead and to tune in with what she is doing, because she is sorting out a few ideas which she will then begin to use in her play. Dancers, musicians, actors and actresses, sportsmen and sportswomen and scientists all need to have time like this to prepare their thoughts and feelings in their heads, and to get their bodies ready before they can move onto their highest level of functioning. Being disturbed during this time will probably mean that the moment is lost and the deep free-flow play (or the dance, piece of music, scientific invention or win in a running race) never develops. High-level play is a fragile thing – it is easily damaged before it gets under way if the atmosphere does not help it along.

During the play, Abigail's mother tells her how, when she was young, she used to pretend she was a sheep. Then she puts the sheepskin rug over Abigail, who likes this idea, and does just that. Adults often begin to remember the play they enjoyed during their childhood as they play with children. It creates a feeling of togetherness between the adult and the child.

Abigail has the right atmosphere for play. She has props which are open enough to allow her play ideas. She has a place to play and people who help her to play and who make time for it to develop without interruption. She begins to free-flow play, using the sheepskin rug as a way of pretending to be a sheep. From this, she moves into creating a play scenario with a story and characters.

She calls her toy lion Jesus. (It is Christmas time and Abigail is brought up as a Christian.) The lion Jesus and the Princess (her Barbie doll) are going to get married. The Princess is preparing herself for the Ball, but gets there late. The lion Jesus marries the toy donkey. One of Jesus's disciples (her toy Dalmatian dog) marries the Princess.

When we imagine, we use our experiences. We rearrange them in new and fascinating ways. That is exactly what Abigail is doing in her play scenario. Several of the stories she has been told or read have been rearranged in new and fascinating ways.

The stories Abigail has used in her play scenario are:

* *Cinderella*
* stories of Jesus
* stories of the disciples
* *The Lion King*
* *One Hundred and One Dalmatians.*

The Barbie doll becomes the Princess character and this is influenced by the story of Cinderella. In the fairy tale, Cinderella is late for the Ball. So is this character, but Abigail has rearranged the story in a new and fascinating way. The soft toys, donkey and dog need characters, so she gives them names from literature and cartoons she knows about, and incorporates them into the play scenario.

This all results in a rich play scenario. It has a story and clearly developed characters. The story has a beginning, middle and end. It takes a dramatic turn or two, but ends happily.

All of the 12 features of play are involved, especially the props and pretend play. Later, when she begins to write, Abigail will be able to pin down her stories and become a creative story writer. This should develop richly by middle childhood, when she is in junior school. But now, she is able to play out the stories she makes with great creativity and enjoyment.

Children often experience intense pleasure as they play. Children are also full of concentration and involvement in their play scenarios. But these are not all happy ones – in their play children may be exploring ideas that worry them.

Many famous people have looked back on their childhood play and have realised how it helped them in later life.

* Richard Feynman, the scientist, had a cart and he liked to put a ball in it. He loved to watch the way the ball rolled about when he moved his cart in different ways as he played. He later studied the way atoms and electrons move about.
* Nelson Mandela remembers playing with friends in the village, on a donkey. He fell off and the children laughed at him. He thought to himself that he would not want to humiliate people when he grew up.
* The Brontë children, Charlotte, Branwell, Emily and Anne, played with lead soldiers. As they reached middle childhood, they began to write down the stories that emerged during their play scenarios, in tiny booklets which they made. These can be seen in the Brontë Museum in Haworth, Yorkshire.

Key message

When we see children beginning to move into play, we can help it along. It will be worth it, as then they will be able to move into their deepest learning. They will use this as a resource as they grow into adults.

Summary

Play helps children to function at the deepest and most wide-ranging levels they can manage.

It is not so much about learning new things, although that is one aspect of it. It is mainly about bringing together, coordinating and applying what has been learned, usually with great effect and success.

If children never feel successful as learners, they will avoid deep learning. Children have to feel that the effort of learning brings some satisfaction. Play helps this to come about. Then they become learners for life, which the children we have observed in this book look all set to do.

REFLECTIVE QUESTIONS FOR YOUR PRACTICE

When you see play beginning to flow, what can you do to support it so that it does not fade before it has got under way? How are you supporting children at play to deepen their play and take it to high levels of thinking?

Give three action strategies that will support the development of play for a baby, toddler and children between the ages of three and five years and three and seven years.

Key messages about learning through play

Bringing together three strands

This book has brought together three strands which are important when exploring the importance of play in early childhood. These are as follows:

1. The traditional view, arising out of the work of late nineteenth- and early twentieth-century pioneers of the early childhood curriculum in the UK, that play is of central importance in helping children to learn.
2. Evidence of a modern kind, that play supports and extends children in their learning, especially when it is well planned.
3. The need to link official documents and legal requirements to the traditions and evidence surrounding early childhood play.

The first two strands help practitioners in the UK and wider world to develop well-planned play, in the home or group setting, as childminders, parents, or staff working in a group. The third strand reminds practitioners of the need to make links from their traditions and from the evidence to incorporate official documents into their work. In this way, practitioners, wherever they are working, can feel that they are connected to other colleagues and are not working in isolation.

This is especially important for reception class teachers in England, or staff who do not yet feel they have sufficient training to be confident in their practice. The three strands help us to look at play so that we can all become more informed about its contribution to learning in early childhood.

Fair play in early childhood practice

Play is complex to understand and it varies enormously:

* in different cultures
* when children have special needs or disabilities
* for boys and girls
* in different families
* with different personalities.

The possibility to play is biologically within every child, but not all children will play.

The right to play is now recognised in the Convention on the Rights of the Child (1989, UNICEF), Article 44. Play is different from recreation and relaxation, which children also need when they have been playing hard.

Fair play for early childhood practice means we need to try to find out more about common features in play because these are part of being a human. We need to explore differences that we can celebrate because they enrich the world.

Observing and describing play

The importance of observation

Observation begins with description and then uses theory and research to analyse and interpret. In this book, the 12 features of play (Bruce, 1991) are used as a window on play, giving us a structure for interpretation. These features have emerged from the work of the pioneers of the early childhood curriculum and recent research and theory.

Observation helps us to become more informed about play. It should deepen our respect, admiration and enjoyment of the way babies, toddlers and young children learn. It should open up our thinking, and never be used to control children's play and learning.

How play makes sense of learning

Play helps children to develop their intelligence in every way.

* It helps children to think through ideas and apply them in all sorts of ways, safely in the world of play.
* It allows children to explore, manage, deal with and control their feelings.
* It encourages children to develop relationships, with their inner selves, others and their universe.
* It is a biological possibility, but it is 'triggered' by people.
* It creates an attitude of mind which brings deep involvement in learning, fosters the desire to learn and to be an adventurous learner.

How play helps develop abstract ideas

Moving from the present to the future and past

As they develop a sense of who they are (identity) and how they are different from other people (theory of mind), children begin to talk or sign and the images in their minds become more mobile. This means that, instead of thinking and feeling in the here and now, they can become increasingly abstract in the way they think, feel and relate to people, events and ideas. This is because abstract thinking opens up possibilities of thinking backwards and forwards.

Play supports the development of creativity and imagination.

Observing, supporting and extending play

Children need places and spaces to play, objects and materials to play openly with, and, most important, people who help them to play.

Planning that supports and encourages play leads practitioners to support and extend children's play through their teaching – a powerful way of helping children learn in early childhood.

Play helps children to make good use of their learning, so that they can use what they know to learn more.

How play helps children to understand other people

In their play, children become more aware of how other people think, feel and relate to each other. They become more sensitive to others, and develop sympathy or empathy (imagining what someone else feels or thinks). Play helps children to work out why and how people think differently from them, as they try out different ways of doing things. Play is a safe way to explore hurting, being hurt, angry or sad, or spreading enjoyment.

Play is the highest form of learning in early childhood

When children free-flow play, alone or with others, they are able to reach their deepest and most wide-ranging levels of learning. They can do their best learning. Learning is only partly about learning new things; it is mainly about using what is already known, in flexible and imaginative ways. A child at play can do this to the full.

Putting what we know into practice

What can practitioners do?

* Enjoy reading or telling stories and poems to children, and singing songs and rhymes with them.
* Play music and watch dances, so that children have ideas about what different kinds of music sound like and realise that there are many ways to dance.
* Make music and dance with children, even if you don't think you can! The adults in this book danced about in the park, kicking leaves in the autumn. This is the basis of rhythm and dance.
* Enjoy looking at nature, and objects and materials together, so that you talk about how things work, animals and the natural world.
* Value the ideas, thoughts and feelings that children have.
* Be relaxed. All of this is indirect teaching of the kind which lasts for life. The learning the children do will be used by them in their play.

* Give children plenty of time for their play.
* Join in, but don't dominate.
* Set up a challenging and exciting environment for play. Visit the park. Play in the garden, and create play scenarios indoors, too.
* Make dens.
* Develop a workshop area, with everything anyone could need for drawing and writing, painting, clay, dough, and construction from found materials and wooden blocks.
* Know when to leave children to develop their own play. Children need time and space to play, so that they can reflect on what they know and have the chance to understand how they think and feel, and relate to people.
* Of course, the possibilities for play are limitless, but they should be informed by the children's own interests.

Useful resources

Siren Films Ltd: Observing Child Development Series
info@sirenfilms.co.uk, www.sirenfilms.co.uk

The following are particularly relevant in relation to play:

* Babies Outdoors: Play, Learning and Development (0–12 months)
* Toddlers Outdoors: Play, Learning and Development (12–14 months)
* Two-Year-Olds Outdoors@ Play, Learning and Development (2–3 years)
* The Wonder Year: First-year development and shaping of the brain
* Learning through Play: The 2- to 4-year old
* Play and Development: The first year
* Pretend Play: 20 months to 7 years
* Exploratory Play: Heuristic play 7–29 months

Bibliography

Albon, D. (2010) 'Postmodern and post-structuralist perspectives on early childhood education', in Miller, L. and Pound, L., *Theories and Approaches to Learning in the Early Years*, Sage: London.

Athey, C. (1990) *Extending Thought in Young Children: A Parent–Teacher Partnership*, Paul Chapman Publishing: London.

Bartholomew, L. and **Bruce**, T. (1994) *Getting to Know You: A Guide to Record-keeping in Early Childhood Education and Care*, Hodder & Stoughton: London.

BBC Radio 4 (1999) 'Tuning into children', presenter Kirsty Wark, resident expert Tina Bruce.

Bergman, A. and **Sackler Lefcourt**, I. (1994) 'Self-other action play: a window into the representational world of the infant', in Slade, A. and Palmer Wolf, D. (eds), *Children at Play: Clinical and Developmental Approaches to Meaning and Representation*, Oxford University Press: Oxford, NY, Toronto.

Blakemore, C. (2001) 'The implications of brain studies for the early childhood curriculum', unpublished lecture given at the RSA, 14 February.

Bowerman, M. (1999) 'Learning how to structure space for language: a cross-linguistic perspective, in Bloom, P., Peterson, M.A., Nadel, L. and Garrett, M.F. (eds), *Language and Space*, MIT: Cambridge, MA.

Bowlby, J. (1953) *Child Care and the Growth of Love*, Penguin: London.

Bruce, T. (1987) *Early Childhood Education*, Hodder & Stoughton: London.

Bruce, T. (1991) *Time to Play in Early Childhood Education*, Hodder & Stoughton: London.

Bruce, T. (1996) *Helping Young Children to Play*, Hodder & Stoughton: London.

Bruce, T. (2000) 'What do brain studies tell us about how to develop a curriculum of quality for young children?' *Early Childhood Practice: the Journal for Multi-Professional Partnerships*, 2, 1, 60–75.

Bruce, T. (2004) *Developing Learning in Early Childhood*, Paul Chapman Publishing Ltd: London.

Bruce, T. (ed.) (2010a) *Early Childhood: A Student Guide*, 2nd edn, Sage: London.

Bruce, T. (2010b) 'Froebel today', in Miller, L. and Pound, L. (eds), *Theories and Approaches to Learning in the Early Years*, Sage: London.

Bruce, T. (2011a) *Cultivating Creativity in Babies, Toddlers and Young Children*, 2nd edn, Hodder Education: London.

Bruce, T. (2011b) *Early Childhood Education*, 4th edn, Hodder Education: London.

Bruce, T., **McNair**, L. and **Wyn Siencyn**, S. (2008) 'I made a unicorn: open-ended play with blocks and simple materials', www.communityplaythings.co.uk.

Bruce, T., **Meggitt**, C. and **Grenier**, J. (2010b) *Child Care and Education*, 5th edn, Hodder Education: London.

Bruce, T. and **Spratt**, J. (2011c) *Essentials of Literacy from 0–7: A Whole Child Approach to Communication, Language and Literacy*, 2nd edn, Sage: London.

Calvin, W. (1997) *How Brains Think*, Weidenfeld and Nicolson: London.

Carter, R. (1998) *Mapping the Mind*, Weidenfeld and Nicolson: London.

Christie, J. (ed.) (1991) *Play and Early Literacy Development*, State University of New York Press: New York.

Core Experiences for the Early Years Foundation Stage (2009), initiated by Julian Grenier, www.early-education.org.uk

Corsaro, W. (1979) 'We're friends, right?' Children's use of access rituals in a nursery school, *Language in Society*, 8, 315–36.

Dahlberg, G., **Moss**, P. and **Pence**, A. (1999) *Beyond Quality in Early Childhood Education and Care: Postmodern Perspectives*, Falmer Press: London.

Damasio, A. (2004) *Looking for Spinoza*, Random: London.

Davies, M. (2003) *Movement and Dance in Early Childhood*, 2nd edn, Paul Chapman Publishing Ltd: London.

Duncan, I. (1930) *My Life*, Victor Gollancz: London, p. 280.

Dunn, J. (1988) *The Beginnings of Social Understanding*, Blackwell: Oxford.

Dunn, J. (1991) 'Young children's understanding of other people: evidence from observations within the family', in Fye, K. and Moore C. (eds), *Theories of Mind*, Lawrence Erlbaum: Hillsdale, NJ.

Elfer, P. and Grenier, J. (2010) 'Personal, social and emotional development', in Bruce, T., *Early Childhood: A Student Guide*, Sage: London.

Feynman, R. (1990) *What Do You Care What Other People Think? Further Adventures of a Curious Character*, Unwin Hyman: London.

Forbes, R. (2004) *Beginning to Play: From Birth to Three*, Open University Press: Maidenhead.

Gardner, H. (1993), *Frames of Mind*, 2nd edn, Fontana/HarperCollins: London.

Goddard-Blythe, S. (2000) *The Well Balanced Child: Movement and Early Learning*, Hawthorn Press: Stroud.

Goldschmied, E. and Jackson, S. (1993) *People Under Three*, Routledge: London.

Goouch, K. and Lambirth, A. (2007) *Understanding Phonics and the Teaching of Reading: Critical Perspectives*, Open University Press, McGraw-Hill Education: London.

Gopnik, A., Meltzoff, A. and Kuhl, P. (1999) *How Babies Think*, Weidenfeld and Nicolson: London.

Greenland, P. (2010) 'Physical development', in Bruce, T., *Early Childhood: A Student Guide*, 2nd edn, Sage: London.

Gura, P. (1996) *Resources for Early Learning: Children, Adults and Stuff*, Hodder & Stoughton: London.

Holland, P. (2003) *We Don't Play with Guns Here*, Open University Press: Maidenhead.

Hyder, T. (2005) *War, Conflict and Play*, Open University Press: Maidenhead.

Isaacs, S. (1930) *Intellectual Growth in Young Children*, Routledge and Kegan Paul: London.

Isaacs, S. (1933) *Social Development in Young Children*, Routledge and Kegan Paul: London.

Kallialla, M. (2006) *Play Culture in a Changing World*, Open University Press: Maidenhead.

Lane, J. (2008) *Young Children and Racial Justice*, National Children's Bureau: London, from www.ncb.org.uk

Leach, P. (1997) *Your Baby and Child: The Essential Guide for Every Parent*, 3rd edn, Penguin Books: Harmondsworth.

MacNaughton, G. (2000) *Rethinking Gender in Early Childhood Education*, Paul Chapman Publishing: London.

Malaguzzi, L. (1996) *The One Hundred Languages of Children: the Exhibit*, Reggio Children: Italy.

Malloch, S. and Trevarthen, C. (2010) *Communicative Musicality: Exploring the Basis of Human Companionship*, Oxford University Press: Oxford.

Mandler, J. (1999) 'Preverbal representation and language', in Boom, P., Peterson, M.A., Nadel, L. and Garrett, M.F. (eds), *Language and Space*, MIT: Cambridge, MA.

Manning Morton, M. and Thorp, M. (2003) *Key Times for Play: The First Three Years*, Open University Press: Maidenhead.

Matthews, J. (2003) *Drawing and Painting: Children and Visual Representation*, Paul Chapman Publishing Ltd: London.

Matthews, J. (2010) *Starting from Scratch: The Origin and Development of Expression, Representation and Symbolism in Human and Non-human Primates*, Psychology Press: London.

May, H. (2000) '"Mapping" some landscapes of colonial global childhood', unpublished keynote address at the 10th Conference of the European Early Childhood Research Association on Quality of Early Childhood Education, London, August 29–September 1.

McKellar, P. (1957) *Imagination and Thinking*, Cohen and West: London.

Montessori Schools Association (2008) *Guide to the Early Years Foundation Stage in Montessori Settings*, Montessori St Nicholas Charity: London.

Moyles, J. (ed.) (2010) *The Excellence of Play*, 2nd edn, Open University Press: Buckingham, Philadelphia.

Nielsen, L. (1992) *Space and Self: Active Learning by Means of the Little Room*, Sikon (available from RNIB, National Education Centre, Garrow House, 190 Kensal Road, London W10 5BT).

Orr, R. (2003) *My Right to Play*, Open University Press: Maidenhead.

Piaget, J. (1962) *Play, Dreams and Imitation in Childhood*, Routledge and Kegan Paul: London.

Rice, S. (1998) 'Luke's story', in Dwyfor Davies, J., Gamer, P. and Lee, J. (eds), *Managing Special Needs in Mainstream Schools: the Role of the SENCO*, David Fulton Publishers: London.

RNIB (1995) *Play It My Way*, HMSO: London.

Rogoff, B., Mosier, B., Mistry, J. and Goncu, A. (1998) 'Toddlers' guided participation with their caregivers in cultural activity', in Woodhead, M., Faulkner, D. and Littleton, K. (eds), *Cultural Worlds of Early Childhood*, Routledge in association with the Open University: London, New York.

Rubin, Z. (1983) 'The skills of friendship', in Donaldson, M., Grieve, R. and Pratt, C. (eds) *Early Childhood Development and Education,* Blackwell: Oxford.

Talmy, L. (1999) 'Fictive motion in language and "caption"', in Bloom, P., Peterson, M., Nadel, L. and Garrett, M., *Language in Space*, Bradford Books, MIT Press: Cambridge MA, London.

Taplin, J.T. (2010) 'Steiner Waldorf early childhood education offering a curriculum for the 21st century', in Miller, L. and Pound, L., *Theories and Approaches to Learning in the Early Years*, Sage: London.

Tovey, H. (2007) *Playing Outdoors: Spaces and Places, Risks and Challenge*, Open University Press: Maidenhead.

Trevarthen, C. (1998) 'The child's need to learn a culture', in Woodhead, M., Faulkner, D. and Littleton, K. (eds), *Cultural Worlds of Early Childhood*, Routledge: London.

United Nations Convention (1990) *The Rights of the Child.*

Vygotsky, L. (1978) *Mind in Society: the Development of Higher Psychological Processes*, Harvard University Press: Cambridge, MA.

Whiting, B. and Edwards, C. (1992) *Children in Different Worlds: The Formation of Social Behaviour*, Harvard University Press: Cambridge, MA.

Winnicott, D. (1974) *Playing and Reality*, Penguin: Harmondsworth.

Index